The New Plan A

Work to become; not to acquire

RAJESHWARI
GEETA

INDIA • SINGAPORE • MALAYSIA

Notion Press

Old No. 38, New No. 6
McNichols Road, Chetpet
Chennai - 600 031

First Published by Notion Press 2018
Copyright © Rajeshwari & Geeta 2018
All Rights Reserved.

ISBN 978-1-64324-923-0

This book has been published with all efforts taken to make the material error-free after the consent of the author. However, the author and the publisher do not assume and hereby disclaim any liability to any party for any loss, damage, or disruption caused by errors or omissions, whether such errors or omissions result from negligence, accident, or any other cause.

No part of this book may be used, reproduced in any manner whatsoever without written permission from the author, except in the case of brief quotations embodied in critical articles and reviews.

Contents

Praises . . . . *v*
Acknowledgements . . . . *ix*
Foreword . . . . *xiii*
Preface . . . . *xix*

Chapter 1:   Women and Mid Life Career Challenges 1
Chapter 2:   Need for a Break 9
Chapter 3:   Identifying the Career That Suits You 21
Chapter 4A: The Process of a Career Change 37
Chapter 4B: Back to School 63
Chapter 5:   Is Academics More Suited for Women? 93
Chapter 6:   Corporate vs Academia 95
Chapter 7:   Back to Corporate 107

Conclusion *125*
Appendix 1 . . . . *129*
Appendix 2 . . . . *135*
Afterword *145*
References *147*
Webliography *149*

Praises

Mr Vinodkumar Gopinath
Former – CTO, Managing Director – Novatium Solutions
Current – School teacher, Chennai.

I loved what I was doing. Not just during the first year of my career, but even a day prior to making the shift. So why and when did the New Plan A replace my original Plan A?

Personally, three factors pushed me to the new path. First, I discovered my interest in teaching. Second, I thought teaching future generations is a good way to 'give back' to society. Third, the monotonous pattern in my corporate career wanted me to explore something different. And this gave the timing of change while the first two gave me the direction of change.

On reading Rajee's writings, I realise that I am not different from many others who have made such a move. It is fascinating and almost mirrors what I went through – from the tentative first steps to now walking confidently into a classroom filled with 30 screaming kids. It's been a quite a journey!

Mrs Lalitha Balakrishnan
Chief Finance Officer
Sword Global (India) Pvt. Ltd.

The title of the book The New Plan A signifies that it is a "New Plan" all over again.

Many women professionals are quite apprehensive to take a break, pursue studies and come back to their stream again. Various factors, such as economics, career growth, acceptability, etc., contribute to this hesitation. This book breaks the barrier to showcase two professionals who have taken a break and studied further after which one got back to corporate life and the other pursued her career in academics. I am sure this book will give people the confidence and insight into various fears attached to the mid life career break and change over. I wish them all the best in their chosen paths. May their tribe grow and bring in more women to the forefront.

Mr Muralidharan Rajasekaran
Former – The Times Group 22 years
Current – Restauranteur, Mumbai.

I am glad that a book has been written on this much-required topic of career change around mid life. I worked with the Times Group for 22 years before I decided to switch to becoming a restaurateur, and the decision was not easy…

While I identified that my passion lay in the food business, becoming an entrepreneur has had its own set of challenges – right from financial to convincing family members to learning a new skill set.

Rajee and Geeta's book gives insights into how to know whether it's time for a career change, what to look for and how to transition into a new career – all of which struck a chord with me. Good luck to Rajee and Geeta. I am sure this book will be a big success!

Dr Sheela Vishwanath
She holds a Doctorate in Medical Microbiology from the University of Mumbai. She has been successfully managing a polyclinic for over 20 years now – where she consults people on healthy lifestyle choices and effective weight management.

Life is about change at every stage and many a times the choice to follow the heart over the head gives lot more happiness and satisfaction. Having said that, mid life career shift is often viewed with much skepticism. This book by Rajee and Geeta not only debunks the myths, but also chalks out a clear plan as to how you can take the big step forward. A lot of thinking and coordinated effort has gone into bringing out the details in the book. A must read for those out there who believe in the "power" of change. After all, you are never too old to reinvent yourself, right??

Acknowledgements

Geeta

Both Rajee and I had taken a break from our respective corporate careers to figure out what we wanted to do next. We were pursuing our PhDs and we frequently discussed mid life career conflicts. The idea for this book germinated in my mind in one of the random conversations we had, and I am thankful to Rajee for that.

I am extremely grateful to my father and my sisters for always believing in me and to Akshay, Abhishek, Nethra and Navya for bringing immense joy to my life and for just being the way they are.

I am grateful to my brothers-in-law, extended family and close circle of friends for patiently listening to me and putting up with my idiosyncrasies.

My special thanks are also due to Ramesh and Dr Krishna Prasanna for their encouragement and feedback.

I am grateful to Jalaja for supporting me when I re-started my corporate career.

My thanks are also due to my company which provided the much-needed support and freedom.

I would also like to applaud all those amazing working women out there for their "never say die" attitude.

Above all, I am eternally indebted to my mother who continues to live in my heart.

Acknowledgements

Rajeshwari

The idea for this book came during a conversation with my friend and co-author, Dr Geeta Ramanathan, when we were analyzing academia versus corporate, post our respective PhD stints. As we discussed, we felt there was enough material to provide for a book and the subject is of great interest to people in corporate, as many consider switching to academia, at some point in their lives. So it is to Geeta that my first acknowledgement is due.

Post the genesis of the idea, there have been many hiccups personally that kept delaying the writing of this book from my side. My father passed away and I moved to Chennai to be with my mother. It is my parents' blessings that have carried me so far.

The institution that I am a part of right now, Great Lakes Institute of Management, provided me with the conducive ambience to write this book. I am also grateful to Mr Sridar Natarajan, Dean Chennai Business School, Prof Pingali Venugopal, XLRI and Dr L P Sai, IIT Madras – who have all helped me in my journey as an academician. Of course, I continue to derive my strength from close friends and family and my acknowledgements are all due to them. My son Rishi provides me with the needed joy and motivation to always rise above the mundane and do something different – thanks dear for that!

Finally, all Glory to the Almighty who is guiding me in every step of my life.

Foreword

Dr Saundarya Rajesh
Founder-President-AVTAR Group

I was 22 when I landed my first corporate job. As a fresh MBA graduate, the job was everything I wanted it to be – promising, challenging, with rightly-measured incentives for the meritorious, and everything in between. A complete package that I thoroughly enjoyed tackling by virtue of (what some may call) being "career-driven." As for me, it was all that and more. Career for me (like many of us women), meant having an intellectual challenge to face every day, having an adrenaline surge that pushed me for success, a set of peers and colleagues to work with and share more than just target numbers and most definitely the economic freedom. I was like a fish in water – completely enjoying my swim through the deep blue.

Well, and then came the halt. The 3M's that derail most women's careers happened to me – Marriage, Maternity and Motherhood. While I thought that it was a question of getting a little flexibility into my work life, my company was not ready for such a "hard" decision. I had to choose between a family and a career, and the two little feet that kicked on my lap made decisions easy.

I never regretted the decision to quit my job and be with my family when they needed me. It was instinctive for me to take that break and be a full-time mother for my child. But as my child grew, I increasingly became aware of an emptiness that was gnawing at me from within, a growing need to get back to my career. I was very clear that I wanted a job, my financial freedom and scope for continuous intellectual challenge – the entire package! I tried my hand at HR consulting, teaching, radio production and face-painting (yes, I did that!) after which I finally started my own entrepreneurial venture – AVTAR.

Those 4 years of my life were life-altering. It gave me time to think and realise my own potential and understand my bigger purpose. It taught me to not take things for granted, to strive hard and push my limits to achieve what I want. It opened me to my own realities – of what I really desired for in life. I wanted the challenges, and I wanted time for my family. I was very clear about my choices, and I set my career path to give me what I aspired for.

AVTAR has been everything that I wanted in my professional life. It has thrown up the most challenging of problems, which I thoroughly enjoy tackling. It has been a series of eye-openers that have taught me some of the most crucial lessons that I am eternally grateful for. It has been a way to serve a higher purpose in life; all in all, lots of moments of glory, pride, success and ways to live life on-the-edge.

On the other hand, it also moulded me to be a better person in my personal life. I would say that I am more grounded and centred today than I was a couple of decades ago. Having invested my heart and soul into my ventures, I am proud to say that today, work and personal life for me aren't two different worlds. Both just seamlessly flow into each other and is one unified whole. There is no question of balancing one against the other – just the pure joy of living it all up!

48% of India's working women quit their jobs at the altar of motherhood, never to return to work. Taking a break is almost a natural part of a woman's career – be it for marriage, maternity, mobility, elder care or taking care of their kids' education. And then some others don't choose to break and try to balance it all. Mid life choices are crucial. It is important to understand your priorities and your own desires from life. It is that part of your life which can decide the rest of your life and that of all the people around you.

Inspired from the life-experiences of two very different personalities, both with years of corporate life who took a break and pursued their PhD – one who chose to move to academics and the other who chose to return to corporate life – this book will be an eye-opener for those of you who are struggling with these realities every day. It deals with a woman professional's perennial conundrum – should I aspire for it all?

The New Plan A is a road-map for those that are lost in their pursuit for that perfectly integrated life, a guide to those who realise they want to choose alternative paths (or then, maybe not) to encounter success and a checklist for those already on the path to choosing alternate career paths. The book will provide clarity to everyone that is looking to make that critical choice in their life. It promises to be more than just a good read; it is an invitation to some self-introspection that can be transformative. Here's to a life of great possibilities. May you grow to the fullest of your potential!

(Dr Saundarya Rajesh is the creator of India's first ever second career service for women professionals, which today has assisted over 30,000 women. She has been felicitated by the President of India with the #100 Women Achiever Award and Niti Aayog's 25 Women Transforming India Award for her work in increasing women's workforce participation in India.)

Foreword

Ms Revathy
Actor, Director-Indian Film and Entertainment industry

Mid life career change or break is contemplated among women irrespective of the vocation. It is not limited to corporates. Even in movies, interesting roles dry up for women once they touch 30. Mid life concerns set in for women in celluloid much earlier than in corporates.

Middle age ladies are not glamorous according to Indian cinema. it is a sudden transformation for Indian women actors – they become mother, sister, *bhabhi*, etc. There are scant roles in Indian cinema for middle-aged women, because they feel a middle-aged women doesn't have an interesting character. This overnight transition from playing a heroine to a star to playing the hero's mother can be both daunting and trifle demeaning. We need to navigate this phase which can be demoralising.

Stereotypes abound everywhere. Girls under 30 with an hour glass figure, fair, beautiful, well endowed are much more in demand. Just as in corporate, even in movies a woman is perceived to be a good second line to men.

Given the profile of the authors, their range and their experience makes this book seem like a logical outcome. Their similarities as well as their diversity lends a unique flavour to the book.

I am elated that Rajee and Geeta have decided to share their journey with others, especially career women, who experience self-doubt, confusion and are sceptical to take the next steps when faced with mid life career challenges. The book provides valuable insights and inputs.

I had never planned to become an actress. But when I was offered a chance, I decided to give it a shot and got hooked for life. Sometimes, one needs a nudge in the right direction and the guts to take a leap of faith to discover what one truly desires and aspires. I also acted as a mother fairly early on in my career which could have been professional hara-kiri. This was against conventional thinking but I choose to steer my own path and hold my own in the male dominated film industry. I managed to carve a niche for myself amid all odds as I stuck to my core of playing meaty substantial roles.

I too had to reinvent and recharge myself. I blended seamlessly from being an Actor, which remains my core to a producer, director, television actor in my attempt to explore different facets which were a logical extension. In fact the primary reason for me to take up direction was the lack of roles for women in their mid life. I decided that instead of complaining I will direct the movies with the roles I want to act in.

And this is exactly what Rajee and Geeta have tried to convey in their book. I am sure the book will resonate with readers and I am confident it will be of immense value and help to fellow women professionals.

I wish them both the very best.

Preface

This book in spirit is a sequel and has been jointly written by Dr Geeta Ramanathan and me, Rajeshwari. My first book *My Life My Choice* was about 10 real people making the shift from corporate jobs to various careers around the middle of their lives. When that book was published, I got answers to what I was seeking in terms of what career I wanted to pursue for the rest of my professional life, namely academics. I had spent 15 years in a corporate prior to that.

After my move into academics, I realised that I seem to be enjoying my second career, i.e., academics even more than my first. So while academics started out as a Plan B career option, I have decided to name the career 'The New Plan A!' Hence, when I started writing a book about this shift from corporate life to academics, I decided to name it **The New Plan A**.

As mentioned in the beginning, this book is a joint effort between me and Dr Geeta Ramanathan (my PhD colleague at Indian Institute of Technology [IIT] Madras). While mine is a story of transition from corporate life to academics, hers is one of moving from corporate life, getting a PhD and then returning to the corporate world.

Mid life is a challenging phase, particularly for career women when they have to play a balancing act of managing several aspects of their personal and professional lives. Many of them drop off the radar, especially in their forties.

Several studies point out to the low participation of women at senior levels (around 18% only) and how just about only half that number of women are present at middle management levels. The reasons for this phenomenon have been analysed in this book and some insights have been drawn from published literature. The key decision points around mid life for a working woman – the impact on the immediate family, realigning financial goals, managing finances and planning for the next step are also covered in depth.

Dr Geeta has elaborated on the reasons for getting back to a full-time corporate career (despite being fully equipped for an academic career), and this will hopefully enlighten the readers and drive home the point that getting back to a corporate career is not a bad idea.

Similarly, one meets so many people in corporate life across levels – junior, middle and senior – who at some point of time in their lives want to move to teaching as a profession. Hence, this aspect of career movement from corporate to academics has also been covered in this book. These 2 careers together make up for a high chunk of the workforce and, hence, the issues highlighted should resonate with many.

However, we are aware that the subject of *career shift* has been dealt with before and the decision itself is not particularly daring or novel anymore, which is why we have also tried to focus on the interim period of *the break* between careers. Both of us have described the process of taking a break, evolving through the period and arriving at what it takes to define our professional identities at the end of a career break. Hopefully this will resonate with many women readers.

Many women never return to work after a break, largely because of inadequate support systems, mentoring systems and so on. So this aspect of *how to deal with a career break* will provide some insights to them.

Though there are similarities between the 2 career shift stories (corporate and academics), there are also some clear differences. The similarities pertain to our educational qualifications, but the variances in our stories will give the readers a more enriching experience.

What to expect from this book?

In today's world, careers form a significant part of our identities and hence our lives. Therefore, to start with, we have identified some *indicators or signals* that will tell you in advance that it's time to make a change in your careers. We have covered these as a list in detail. This will help you understand whether you are going through these stages.

Of course, there is no need to panic and rush to conclusions regarding one's second career. In fact, it was mentioned clearly in the first book that there is NO NEED to change careers mid-way through life if you are already pursuing something that you enjoy. The crisis may be temporary and it just needs some thought or clarification to get back on track.

The most important part of this book arguably is to *identify which career suits you*. It is a not a straightforward decision. It depends on personal, professional, environmental and circumstantial factors. Many of these are discussed. There is also some formal approach that is outlined so that the decision is more robust. If any of you are able to have a personal takeaway from this section regarding the choice of your second careers, we would be very happy.

Moving on, the next step of *actually going about the career change* has been described. What are the triggers, barriers and incentives? What are the challenges you may face? The intention is to make it a *one-stop checklist* for those who are seriously contemplating a change.

The last couple of sections in this book are for those who view this book as a keepsake reference. Original primary research findings with some women who are going through the transition have been explained in detail.

Overall at the end of reading this book, we sincerely hope you will know whether you want to change careers around mid life, and if so, which career (corporate or academics) you would want to choose and how you would go about it. If you are looking at corporate or academics in particular, you should definitely gain a deeper understanding. As Winston Churchill said, *"Success is not final, failure is not fatal: it is the courage to continue that counts."*

Happy reading ☺.

Chapter 1

Women and Mid Life Career Challenges

Women participation in the workforce has grown by leaps and bounds over the last few decades. However, women's role in the workforce, especially around mid life, changes when they give birth to children or have aged parents to care for. They face many challenges in managing their conflicting responsibilities. The focus of this book is on women because they are considered the primary child nurturers/caregivers who process this experience uniquely.

There are a substantial number of women in middle management today. They are in their midlives and achieving a work–family balance tends to be a serious issue for many of them. *Mid-career* is defined as a transition period of intra-career role adjustment. It is that period in one's life when one's values are deeply evaluated and there is a lot of introspection that may lead to seeking more meaning out of life.

This time period allows individuals to analyse their lives and move deeply and holistically before resuming their career journey. According to Cabrera (2007), 47% of women stop working at some point of time in their career, and mid life is the highest point when this happens. In 2003, New York Times Magazine, carried an article on the opt-out revolution that talked about how women decide to opt out of careers around mid life to fulfil domestic responsibilities.

Today *career gappers*[1] and *grey gappers*[2] are increasing and are expected to increase further. According to UK media reports, more than half of career gappers were in their mid-30s or older in 2013 when compared to a meagre 8% in 2012.

Gender diversity in corporate leadership

There are several barriers impeding a woman's journey upwards on the corporate ladder. Despite an increasingly higher number of women graduating every year, their representation in the top echelons of management in corporates remains abysmally low. According to the findings of a new study by Grant Thornton titled *International Business Report*, the position of women in senior positions in the Indian workforce fell from 19% in 2013 to 14% in 2014.

According to another study by Mckinsey & Co., only 5% of working women in India make it to senior leadership positions in the corporate sector as compared to the global average of 20%.

---

[1] People who take time off from work: breaks, career breaks, etc.
[2] People over 55 who take extended periods of time off to go travelling to distant and exciting places

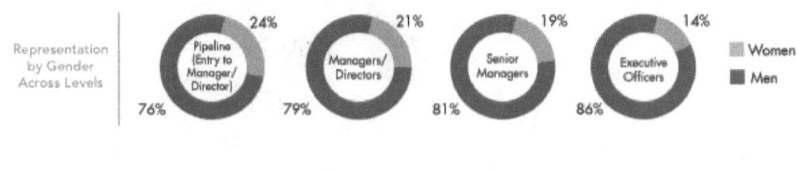

Figure 1: Representation of women in the corporate hierarchy

Women continue to be under-represented in board and senior management positions and the disparity has been growing. As per another Grant Thornton report, the industries where women are most likely to progress into senior management positions are education, social services and healthcare as they are considered to be more amenable and hospitable to women leaders than others.

In Indian companies, 'HR Director' (21%) is the most common role filled by women in senior positions. Many successful women end up in roles in human resources, corporate communications and investor relations that are important yet don't serve as a gateway to the C-Suite. As per *Catalyst*, "Women hold only 7.7% of board seats and just 2.7% of board chairs. The industries with the highest percentage of women on boards are technology, media and telecommunications."

Women have been increasingly opting out of the corporate race at an alarming rate and are becoming entrepreneurs or gravitating towards non-traditional roles such as teaching, NGOs and part-time jobs which offer them better family time. As they grow up the hierarchy, they feel isolated and burdened by the dual requirements, one of meeting their career aspirations and the other of their domestic responsibilities.

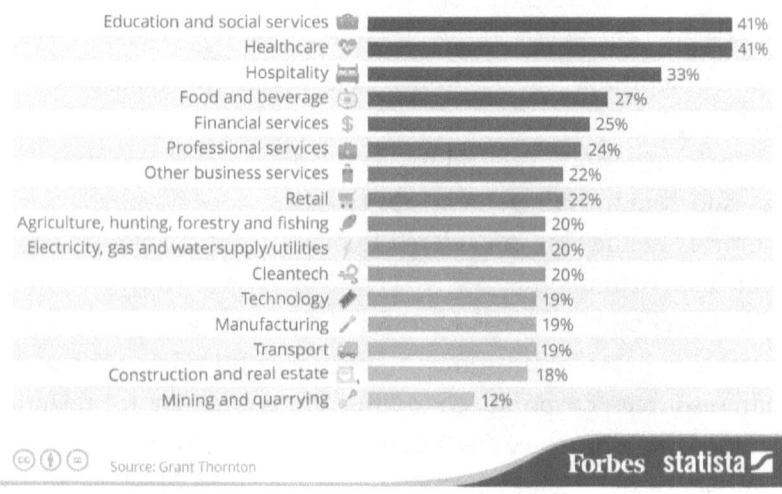

Figure 2: Demographics of senior women leaders across sectors

Career interruptions due to childbirth, child rearing, parental care, other domestic responsibilities and the societal expectation for women to play a supportive role all place them at a disadvantage in the male-dominated corporate environment. As per the Gender Diversity Benchmark Survey for both 2011 and 2014 by Community Business (non-profit organisation), India had the highest dropout rate for women across all levels. In the 2014 survey, it was reported that in markets such as India and China, women were dropping out due to several traditional and societal influences, one of the strongest being *daughterly guilt* which, surprisingly can far outweigh *maternal guilt*.

While day care or crèches for children have become acceptable, day care or institutionalised care for the elderly is a taboo topic and is not acceptable culturally or socially. Moreover, while domestic help or extended family support is easier for childcare, for elderly care and especially ailing elderly care, such options are not readily available or viable. These interruptions further hamper their career progression. Due to this, women are more likely to have non-linear career paths.

Despite being equally or more qualified, several women also take up less demanding jobs as their value is underestimated. Several senior women have reported that in business meetings they have often been mistaken for secretaries.

According to Booz & Co. 2012, investing in women leaders has positive effects on a country's gross domestic product (GDP) and on the welfare of future generations as women reinvest a greater amount on their children's education. While women's lack of representation at senior management positions is universally acknowledged throughout the business world and there is widespread acceptance that a lot needs to be done, the ground realities are at striking odds with these views. A 2014 report revealed that by having flexible workplaces, women's career aspirations increased by nearly 30 per cent and the retention of women improved by almost 40 per cent (CEB, 2014).

Academic theories on careers

There are various theories on career management in academic literature. According to *the scarcity theory,* personal resources such as time, energy and attention are limited, and when there is a conflict of roles, the lesser important role ends up getting lesser resources. Conflict occurs when the demand from one role (home, work, personal, family, etc.) interferes with another. In this case, the woman who assumes the primary caretaker's responsibility has to divide her resources between work and family.

The *kaleidoscopic career model (KCM)* emphasises the importance of authenticity, balance and challenge at various stages of one's career. In the mid-career stage, balance dominates for women and since they are 'relational', they make career decisions based on the impact on others, e.g. family. This may even lead them to being self-employed, change jobs or pursue higher education.

Since women seem to derive satisfaction by combining their work and family aspirations, it is important to understand the factors that will enable them to return to their careers. Far from giving up on their career aspirations, some women around mid life seek a high quality work role that can allow them to pursue a satisfying family role, resulting in a feeling of achieving greater meaning out of life. Developing competencies that will help them stay relevant seems a priority for such women.

Boundaryless careers allow women to make drastic interruptions in their work life. They may learn a new skill, reflect on what is truly important to them and later return with a greater career zest. This requires *know-how*, i.e., competencies and networks, and many women who take a break feel inadequate on these fronts.

There has been a lot of research on why women take a career break in the first place. The various reasons include child rearing (the mommy track), engaging in more family time, caring for the aged (the daughter track) and some push factors such as perceived lack of advancement opportunity, harassment and disdain for corporate culture.

The limited women representation at the top in corporates also implies that there is insufficient role modelling for other women to follow. Social capital is imperative for women to reach the top, and this means that informal networking, if absent, affects their chances of returning to work.

Finally, organisational culture is considered a very masculine trait – fiercely competitive, power games being played, political, etc. – and these deter women, especially around middle to later stages in life when they seek balance and authenticity. However, it has been identified that women are able to build long-term relationships better with customers; they stay longer in an organisation and are better brand advocates for their companies. Given all these, it would be very important to know what will make them come back to work.

Corporate working women opine that it is imperative for companies to extend support systems for a woman's career development in her 20s/early-30s and career advancement in her mid-30s/40s. Many Scandinavian countries like Sweden and Denmark have laid down policies that strengthen a family set-up and allow the working couple to focus on their respective careers while the State looks after the children through a well-established childcare system.

It is obvious therefore that in a developing country like India, the government can play an important part in facilitating women's re-entry to work; campaigns, policies, ministry announcements, etc., can be very useful. In such countries, the government needs to take several measures and float policies to address this issue. Very few organisations, however, have addressed the need for facilitating re-entry in any concerted manner; instead, the solutions to this problem have been found largely by the individuals themselves.

However, this will be increasingly inadequate considering the impact such a huge women force can potentially have on the country's economy. There are also other factors like social, cultural or personal that may aid in this decision of re-entry into their careers.

Career renewal

Earlier, one job was probably equal to one career. Not anymore. In the social context of the 1950s and through the mid-1960s, changing one's career after the age of 30 or so was a relatively infrequent occurrence. In more recent times, the impetus for individual mid-career re-evaluation and subsequent change may be linked, in part, to societal changes and opportunities. For example, widespread automation and, more recently, corporate downsizing have eliminated innumerable industrial, white-collar and professional jobs and forced many to consider mid-career changes. In addition, second incomes from women entering the workforce have reduced the financial strain on some families, thereby diminishing the absolute need for job stability and increasing the opportunity for taking risks.

A review of mid life transitions pointed out that 'social class' is more responsible for determining the distinct stages of adult development as compared to universal experience. The mid life crisis may represent a flight to avoid or deny the experience of stagnation. The 35–55 years age span is a period of rebirth wherein "men leave the compulsive unreflective busywork of their occupational apprenticeships and once more become explorers of the world within." This stage is also called *second adolescence* because there is a renewed interest in sexual expression, a heightened sense of idealism and less willingness to sacrifice leisure and family pursuits on the altar of ambition. In this period, the exploration journeys are likely to be daring and innovative in planning new career pathways. This is termed *career renewal*.

The way women deal with their entry into mid life primarily depends on how they prepare themselves for the change during early adulthood. Women who had new goals and those who risked making important changes in their lives showcased a more positive outlook than women who had not prepared themselves for middle age.

So how exactly does the entire process of career change take shape in the mind? Let's explore this further in the next chapter.

Chapter 2

Need for a Break

"The chief cause of unhappiness is trading what you want most for what you want right now."

– Zig Ziglar

People generally start evaluating their lives when they hit the dreaded age of 40. But what age qualifies as mid life exactly? The definition of mid life has definitely changed over the years. It can happen around 45, 35 or not until 55. It depends on how you plan your career and manage your life. It is in our hands to let a mid life crisis remain a mere psychological term rather than have it affect our lives.

Jonathan Rauch wrote a cover story in 2014 about the "U-shaped happiness curve," a phenomenon propounded by economists Andrew J. Oswald and David G. Blanchflower. As they noted: "Even after controlling for differences in wealth, education, and location, people's general contentment hits a low point in their 40s before rebounding in their 50s." Oswald and other scholars have found that our job satisfaction suffers a parallel dip in mid-career, only to swoop upward in our 50s and 60s.

The ideal situation in everybody's life is to get a job of their liking and to do it with passion. However, not everyone is lucky, and sometimes due to reasons varying from locational constraints, health issues, childcare or elderly care, one takes up a job which would probably be a 2nd or 3rd choice.

Often, people take up a job in which they are selected rather than take up a job of their liking and this causes frustration.

Sometimes you secure a job in the company of your liking but you may need to grapple with a monster of a boss, low salary, no clarity on your growth trajectory, wicked co-workers, pointless meetings, etc. Look around and this a common refrain of people trapped in unhappy jobs. Reasons for quitting a job vary from:

- Low pay
- High stress
- No work-life balance
- Bad boss
- Rigid work schedules
- No opportunity for advancement
- Boredom at work
- Wanting to give back to the community
- All or some of the above

Nigel Marsh, author of *Fat, Forty, and Fired,* gave a TED talk on achieving work-life balance. One of the most relevant quotes perhaps from the talk was: *"Most people work long, hard hours at jobs they hate that enable them to buy things they don't need to impress people they don't like."* How very true, don't you agree?

The 2 factors which cause the maximum stress at office appear to be cognitive dissonance and prolonged monotony as per popular research. At some stage in their career, especially mid life, several begin to find their career not exciting, challenging and fulfilling enough.

As per a Mercer study of 30,000 employees worldwide in 2011, between 28% and 56% of employees around the globe wanted to leave their jobs. Their study in 2015 revealed that these numbers had increased. Studies also reveal that most people will change careers at least once in their working life.

Work stress has been oft-cited as the reason for people taking breaks. Some feel that a break might just bring back that mojo into their job. Many times, the actual values and ethics and what people are required to do as part of their job are at variance and this causes discontent.

In an April 2013 article in Harvard Business Review (HBR) titled *What job candidates really want: Meaningful work*, Nathaniel Koloc stated that there has been a shift in what job candidates seek today, from a stable, well-paying job to more purposeful work. Having an engaged and happy employee increases productivity and thereby contributes directly to the bottom line. Having disgruntled employees on board is a fact few corporates can afford to ignore.

Recruiting an employee involves costs associated with the recruitment fees and onboarding costs. If the time to settle down is factored, this cost will head upwards. Today, for a majority of job seekers, a purposeful position is more likely to be a deal breaker with a corporate than a paycheck.

Women in particular associate professional success with personal fulfilment, which includes family, friends and relationships. Mainiero and Sullivan (2005) found that women taking an 'off-ramp' during mid-career were particularly driven by the need for balance in their lives. The number of women in top management positions continues to remain very low (Burke and Vinnicombe, 2005) and the glass ceiling which first entered corporate lexicon almost 30 years ago unfortunately still exists. The difference though is that now it is positioned at higher levels in the organisational hierarchy (Altman *et al.*, 2005). The desire to do something 'meaningful' and 'emotionally rewarding' has often led women to join an NGO and non-profit organisations.

Another phenomenon that is prevalent but not deliberated enough is that there are a significant number of women who join the workforce due to their desire or compulsion to contribute to the family income and to simply keep themselves engaged during their idle time. Such women may also drop off the corporate radar once their requirement is met.

As per a study conducted by Avtar Careers, the various stumbling blocks that an Indian woman professional encounters as she treads her career path can be categorised broadly as:

- Cultural
- Social
- Structural
- Personal
- Job role related/professional

Though women's career aspirations are guided by their dreams and desires, they often get moulded by the advice and expectations of family members, their life stage, monetary considerations and their exposure.

There is a possibility that the ennui one experiences in one's job could just be a minor blip which requires stepping back a bit or making minor modifications to one's career. It might be a one-off case of a rough day or a couple of instances of a rough day. It might help to take a couple of days off to de-stress and indulge in some serious introspection.

Maybe one needs a sabbatical, and if the office allows it, one could explore the options available. Quitting may not be required in all instances. It might help to talk to your Human Resources (HR) department or your boss. One may like the work but not the environment. A job switch might solve the problem. After all, one might dislike and not want the job but they might need one.

Stephen Stills, the American singer, penned a verse which can be paraphrased as follows:

If you can't be in the job you love...
Love the job you're in (or the way you do it)

One needs to have clarity about what one is actually seeking in a job. Whether the priority is moolah, a good brand, an inspiring boss, a 5-day week, job content, career path, autonomy, growth prospects... it could be anything. If you get it all, you have hit the jackpot. But although ideal, this is a rare scenario. If your energy levels are dipping, you probably need to step back a bit and reenergise yourself to get the zest back into your life. Rebooting your life could be the need of the hour. In an impulsive move, let's not throw out the baby with the bathwater. There is a high possibility that mid life discontent may recede with time.

One possible reason for this to occur could be that for a major part of our lives, we were taught to focus on Intelligence Quotient (IQ), which we flaunted proudly if we had decent scores. Then, close on the heels, emerged the Emotional Quotient (EQ). We were told that EQ is required in equal measures for a well-rounded, wholesome life. But now we are told that even these are not enough and we need PQ a.k.a 'positive quotient.' Our mind is our best friend and can also become our worst enemy. We need to train our mind to look out for the positive aspects and act upon it for our well-being.

One of course wishes that face time were not the criteria for judging one's efficiency or output in an organisation. This becomes a hassle particularly when dealing with emergencies in our personal lives, like for example, taking an elderly family member to the doctor. Most of the docs you need to consult with will invariably have an odd timing of 10–1 or 2–4, which boils down to availing a 'permission' or 'leave.' And despite taking an appointment, one can never estimate when the doctor's consultation will be completed.

Seeking permission from superiors seems like such an obligation and is best avoided. Frequent requests for permissions and leave are also looked down upon by the management. These and more are some of the reasons that leads one to wish for the freedom and flexibility to do as one desires. Further, emergencies arise in work life as well and this unpredictability induces stress and is considered less family-friendly by women. As indicated earlier, women particularly connect professional success with personal fulfilment. A woman's career choices thus are to a major extent influenced by familial circumstances.

Recessions and corporate layoffs are not uncommon these days, especially in the IT, telecom and retail sectors, apart from some start-ups. There was an article in the *Times of India* (TOI) dated 1.5.2017 on how some engineers, especially women, who were placed in blue-chip IT companies were looking for vacancies for teachers' positions at private schools – a job swap which was felt would insulate them from the nasty surprises of an economic slowdown.

To people who fear such instances, well, an article in a magazine stated that *at the end, life is the sum of your experiences, not your possessions*. There was an elderly couple who were stinking rich but always calculated pennies and did a cost-benefit analysis at every stage. The couple died rich, and less than 5 years later, their offspring sold off the house and funded his business with the money and travelled extensively. This reminds one of the popular quote: *"The amount of money that's in your bank at the time of death is the extra work you did which wasn't necessary."*

"I can understand wanting to have millions of dollars; there's a certain freedom, meaningful freedom, that comes with that. But once you get much beyond that, I have to tell you, it's the same hamburger."

— *Bill Gates*

Sometimes people just linger in a perpetual state of dissatisfaction and frustration and ruminate and introspect incessantly without doing anything about it. They have a disproportionate tendency towards inertia rather than change which is defined as the *status quo effect*. Disrupting the status quo and opting to charter a new path is not easy, and not everyone wants to rock the boat.

There is a noticeable pattern in the stories of people who have gone through this career change. Being courageous is just not enough. Making the real career change is quite hard. It's not because people are resisting change. There are many people who have made various attempts at starting a new career but haven't been successful. The actual issue is the way people approach this process.

For example, *most people expect the same things from their second career as they did from their first; this expectation is flawed*. Ideally, the expectation from your second career should evolve over time. Meanwhile, experiment, try out new methods, talk to people and start forming your own identity. This is also referred to as 'working' identity, as one's identity is work in progress. Of course, the other reason it is called so is that it is related to our work lives.

Working identity

The questioning process of whether the career we are in is right for us and, if not, what we want out of a future pushes us to plan and see what we want to do next. However, this 'plan and implement' approach doesn't work for second careers. We need to experiment and learn. The 'test and learn' mechanism says that the only way to defy uncertainty is to make alternative futures more tangible and more doable. Our old identities were acquired through practice. Similarly our new identities will also be formed by experimenting, networking and making sense of the changes. These 3 elements are crucial for successful career changes.

Designing experiments

Delaying the first step is the most common mistake that career changers make. They do not realise that the only way they would figure out their destination is by trying. *The truth is that most of us are scared of the unknown.* Most people start off by getting involved in new activities during weekends and other extracurricular activities.

Designing experiments involves creating these side projects. This helps us to try out our new dream job without having to give up on the current job. Research points that in almost every successful career change, the person was already involved in his new career for some time. The thought is not to jump into something new without giving yourself time to explore the new career.

There are a number of ways through which these experiments can work. Some of the options include taking up freelancing, temporary contracts or advisory work while continuing your present job. You can also enrol in new courses to learn fresh skills. Some people opt to take a break or a sabbatical. These breaks help in getting away from the monotony and involving yourself in new activities.

> **You will never know what is right for you, unless you try**

The power of networks

Networking helps to find the right people who can guide us into being our new self. Most successful career changers have mentors who have helped them take the leap. The irony is that more often than not *strangers are the ones who help us see who we want to be.* Close working relationships are not always where we find refuge during uncertain times. Traversing unknown territories, often through networking, is important to find new careers. A close friend of ours, another career changer, found his mentor in the founder of his company. He believed in his potential as a general manager and eventually helped him do the kind of work he actually wanted to.

Making sense

Surrounded by so much confusion, many of us are looking for validation. We hope for that one thing which will put a stamp on our choices, that one event that would transform our uncertain moves into a rational course. *Making sense* refers to creating our own triggers, events with special meaning and converting them into a story about what we want to become. *Almost every person we know who has changed careers has a story.*

A woman acquaintance, another career changer, who was working as an executive assistant in a start-up was very frustrated with her job. She had her moment of truth when her husband asked her if she was happy because she evidently didn't look happy. That question and that moment made her reconsider what she had been doing.

The *moment of truth* is more of an effect rather than a cause of change. It has been gathered through findings that such moments occur much later in the transition process, after much trial has been done. These defining moments help people make sense of the decisions and changes that they have made.

Often we believe that we need to know exactly what we want to do and then take the plunge. However, for second careers the opposite is true. Firstly we need to try out different things and then finalise it. Doing comes before knowing, 'knowing ourselves' through our first careers, and then figuring out what we need to do next. First act and then think is the sequence followed because who we are and what we do are closely connected. The worst thing to do would be to just consider one career that will change our lives. This never happens in reality.

The new career has to chase you as much as you are chasing it. By the time we are at an age when we start considering a career change, we are filled with various experiences from our work, relationships and other aspects. Now, when we do all this work, it is on our subconscious level without us actually thinking about it and an option for our second career begins to appear. This is mostly a vague picture of what we could possibly do. This vague option starts to become more concrete when we meet people in that area or join discussions that fuel it. So at this point, you only need to pull back, reflect and let the thoughts come to you instead of chasing them aggressively.

Know the 'real' you

Analysing your career and identifying what aspects you like and what you did not is a very satisfying and useful method. However, most often this practice is based on the assumption that it is possible to discover one's true self. But the truth is that none of us actually have that power. There is a high possibility of a career changer being stuck in his dreamland if he goes too deep into introspection. It can have 2 outcomes. Either the dream career never finds a real match in the real world, or we might continue to be emotionally attached to a dream career so much so that we don't even realise that we may have outgrown it.

The ideal way forward is testing the fantasy career for reality and not just introspecting. Knowing oneself is important, but it is the outcome and not the first step in the reinvention process. Reinvention requires us to get the idea out of our heads and to act upon it.

How helpful are family and friends?

In times of uncertainty, we have a natural tendency to look for advice from friends and family. But it has been observed over time that when it comes to reinventing oneself, the people who know us best are more likely to hinder than help us. The intention of course is pure, but they tend to reinforce our old identities that we are trying to shed.

Mentors, co-workers, headhunters, all prove quite unhelpful. When a friend tried brainstorming with his close circle about his career change, all that he got in return further reinstated the belief that he was better off where he was. Typical replies would be "Yes, that sounds very interesting, but you already have a stable job. Do you want to risk that?"

So what is the solution? To make a true break from the past, we need guides who have been there and can understand where we are going. New network circles and professional communities offer the best revelation to see yourself in a new light.

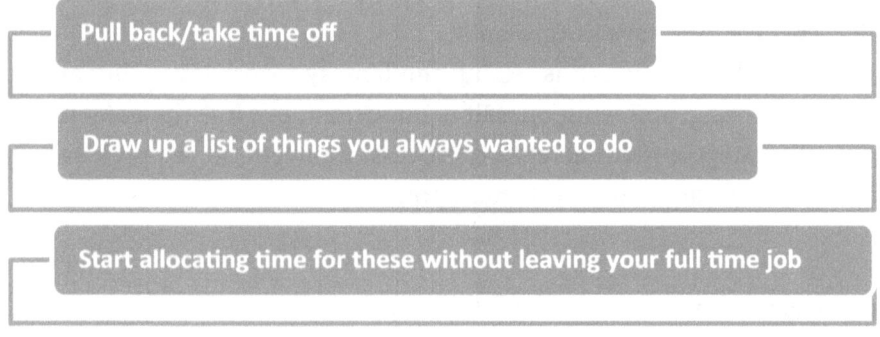

Figure 3: Major steps involved in exploring options

One step at a time…

Tap into your innermost recesses to understand what your real motive or reason for wanting a change is. Which aspects of your current job do you dislike?

If you are disengaged with your current job and previous jobs, the problem may not be the job but might lie with you.

Most of us think that we can directly jump from a desire for a change to a single decision and complete the process of reinvention. However, in reality, trying to jump into big changes too quickly can be counterproductive. Trying to make one big move once and for all can inhibit real change. Taking smaller steps is the key to a successful career change.

Breaking away

When I was working in a corporate, it was just work, work and work on weekdays and sometimes even on weekends. If there was indeed some respite from office work or official calls on weekends, the time was just sufficient to attend to personal chores, watch tripe on TV, catch up with some friends, visit relatives and sleep. Life had begun to resemble a boring timetable. What seemed exciting and challenging in the initial years had become overwhelming. I had degenerated into a cookie-cutter corporate drone.

A 9 to 5 job seemed so passe! Wake up at 6, go for a walk, read the newspaper, complete household chores and then get ready in a jiffy and leave home in a mad rush and then get back home by 7/8/9/10 or the next morning, depending on the urgency of the work. When I worked for consulting firms, working a minimum of 12 hours was the norm rather than an exception. There was no fixed time for lunch or dinner or calling it a day. I was living my life on a loop. I was working on autopilot mode.

While people experience atrophy in their skills when on a sabbatical, I was facing it even while I was working. Was I missing the point here? Or was I suffering from an aspirational deficit? I was probably suffering from 'attention deficit disorder.' Thankfully back then, they didn't have fancy sounding names for these issues or conditions.

I didn't have a roadmap or blueprint to chalk out my corporate strategy when I started out. I lived with the naiveté that since I had enviable grades and I had been selected for my first corporate job in a well-known company through a competitive exam and interview, things would automatically pan out for me. In hindsight, I realise that one of the key skills required in moving up the corporate ladder is to have a plan and to have a strategy, which was missing in my decision-making process.

Yes, never underestimate the power of decision-making. I was often left wondering if there was a seminar or workshop that I had missed along the way because everyone else appeared confident and seemed to know the corporate rules except *moi*.

And so, I was in an extremely unhappy and frustrated phase towards the turn of the century. I badly wanted to quit my job. I was beginning to feel unfulfilled and unchallenged by my work and also under-utilised. The anxiety had increased. But I hung in there to sort out several things. I went into a shell and that affected my career prospects further.

I saw some of my colleagues with absurdly fat pay cheques and bloated paunches doing exceedingly well for themselves but never looking happy and contented. Earlier, I looked at my peers with envy on account of the fat bucks they were earning. Later, I looked at them with pity. Most of them were earning millions of bucks but did not even have the time to spend it. The corporate world seemed dystopian to me. We would postpone and procrastinate and live for the weekends, like weekend warriors.

I wanted to step back and decide what I wanted to do with my life. I wanted to leave my comfort zone, my protective cocoon. Some gleefully wrote my obituary. It was probably *avant-garde* especially for someone to do this in their forties. *I was probably facing a burnout. Maybe I needed a therapist. Was I going through a mid life crisis? Was I afflicted by corporate ennui?*

I was also acutely aware that a career interruption would negatively impact my income and designation should I choose to return to the corporate fraternity. By taking a break, was I running away? Maybe... maybe not.

Which brings us to the next question – How do you identify that particular career that suits you? We will explore this in the next chapter.

Chapter 3

Identifying the Career That Suits You

> A lifetime spent doing something you don't like, is a lifetime wasted

The word career throws up around 1.59 crore results on Google! While most of these searches may not be relevant for the group that is reading this book, the fact remains that there are innumerable career options today. The Oxford dictionary defines *career* as an occupation undertaken for a significant period of a person's life and with opportunities for progress.

Selecting a career for the first time is daunting enough! More often than not, the first careers that we choose are a function of our educational qualifications, peer pressure, parents' expectations and so on. And to do it the second time around is not something easy. In my case, I took a career break of one year after my long15-year corporate stint. This break of one year was not predetermined but eventually it did end up being so.

The first couple of months were very difficult as I was used to a very busy schedule. But suddenly during the break, I had so much free time. Of course there was a home and a child to take care of and that meant building involvement in these aspects, i.e., I had to now start getting into the daily details of home management and my child's daily routine. I had a live-in help who had been with me for a few years. But it was becoming increasingly obvious to me that the way I spent my day was going to change dramatically.

Taking a break implies not too many calls, not many invitations; basically no structure, which might be daunting for some.

During the initial period of this break when you are undergoing the transition, it is better not to conclude anything about your next career. Let time flow and slowly a list will begin to emerge. Keep a journal to record your thoughts. This will be particularly useful at a later stage when you want to refer back to understand how you went through the career change process.

The period just after the career break

There was a period after my corporate career where I suffered from a deep identity crisis. Until then, I had identified myself with being a corporate working woman primarily. So when the corporate association was taken away, I felt a huge emptiness. I strongly felt the need to reinvent myself across other dimensions. So how did I go about it?

Drawing a chart

The starting point was to simply list the roles that I wanted to expand myself on. This included being a mother, being a wife, being a daughter, being a friend and of course taking care of myself, the individual. So I ventured into drawing a chart that was sectioned inside with the various roles. I started breaking down the roles into different aspects and outlining what it took to excel in each of them.

For example, being a daughter meant the following: visiting my parents regularly, taking them for doctor visits, helping my father in administrative work, etc. Similarly, being a mother meant playing an active role in my child's academics, helping him have a network of friend, supervising his extracurricular activities, etc.

The role of the 'individual self' was an important one. I did not want to get lost in playing the other roles so much so that I lost sight of my own self. This particular role was further categorised as fitness, intellectual pursuit, learning a new skill, etc. For another role, that of a 'good friend,' I identified a set of people whom I respected and trusted. I started having regular, conscious interactions with them and spent time with them. I felt that was needed to strengthen my emotional space with like-minded people and enhancing friendships in this area was a source of great comfort.

I completed drawing the chart and displayed it in my bedroom to serve as a constant reminder. It was colourfully done and I believe it provided me with the much-needed focus for the new life that I was embarking upon.

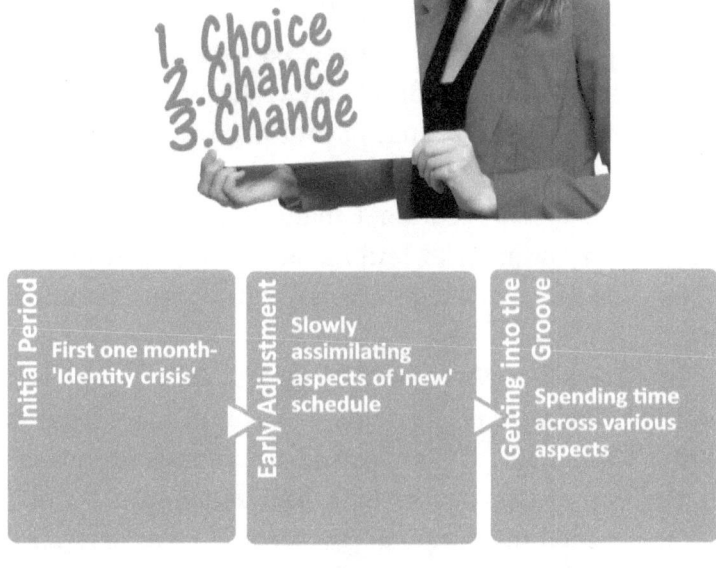

Figure 4: Period immediately post career change

Having a full-time career in sales and marketing meant that I was thinking of my job almost 24/7. It also meant a lot of travel (10–12 days a month) and meetings even on weekends. In effect, work was priority number one and I had very little time left for the family. I had done substantial delegation of my work at home. Now, however, all that had to change.

What did I do differently?

First and foremost, I started spending more time with my son. I became a part of his school circle more closely. I started taking an active, hands-on interest in his daily schedule and made it a point to pick and drop him from school. Also, I began to get more involved in terms of his dietary requirements and physical activities. The idea was to integrate much more into his life, which I believed would provide primary meaning for me at my life stage, and of course, the reasons for my career break.

The more I started doing this, the more my sense of purpose increased. The child always needs the mother the most. The interactive nature of the relationship brought a lot of joy and learning. My child's emotional confidence in school and his happiness levels were visibly improving.

The other aspect of my new routine was closer housekeeping. In addition to doing the daily chores, I started consciously building closer ties with other families and children. One realisation that dawned on me during the phase was the fact that having been in the corporate world for so many years, the aspect of personal relationships with family and friends had been deprioritised. So I made it a point to make a list of people with whom I wanted to build deeper long-term relationships. I consciously drew up a schedule of these people and met them for lunches, dinners, etc.

So my new life primarily comprised these 2 aspects: one of childcare and the other of looking after the home. Both of these are long-term goals where gratification is delayed! Coming from a corporate set-up that rewards or punishes almost instantly, this long wait required a lot of patience. However, it was something that I had chosen and I was determined to see it through fully.

Aspects of 'new' life	How do you feel?	What next?
• Child care taking • Housekeeping	• Sense of purpose • Satisfying/in control	• Understand further requirements • Plan for higher levels of delegation • Use your connections and attend seminars. • Tap into all your networks. Look for referrals and leads.

Figure 5: What next?

Along with getting my personal priorities in place, the question that was bothering me was "What should I do for the rest of my professional life?" After all, I was just 36 years old and felt quite energetic and contribution worthy. But as I have mentioned in my first book, *simple questions do not have simple answers.*

I tried going through the list that I drew up to explore what may interest me as a second career option. In my job as a sales and marketing professional till then, the aspects that I enjoyed were leadership, communication, motivation, conceptual clarity and goal achievement. In spite of the daily pressures of accomplishing targets, I used to look forward to the above aspects. So I asked myself, "Is there a job that would allow me to continue on these aspects but without the corporate context?" There were a couple of options that came to my mind, namely trainer and a public speaker, but I felt that these 2 would still not do justice to my complete potential.

I also observed my parents' hobbies. My father had done his Masters in Literature and my mother was a Classical Arts person. In their free time, my father would read voraciously and my mother dabbled in painting and playing the veena. As an experiment, for a while I took to blogging – it was my way of giving written form to my thoughts. It also strengthened my writing skills and may unknowingly have sown the seeds for authorship! I also took to painting very diligently. In fact, I enrolled myself in formal classes and completed my first mural art painting in 6 months. This gave me a huge sense of accomplishment in addition to building my patience as a virtue, much needed at that point in time.

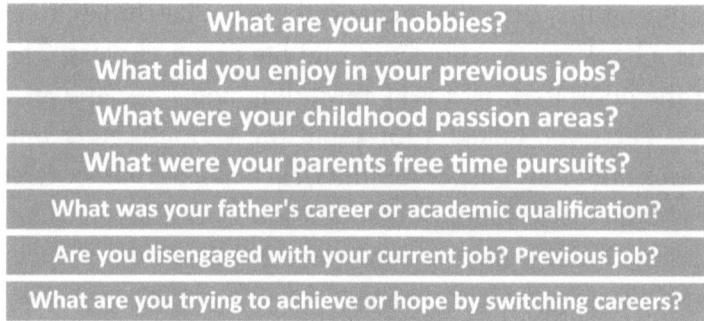

Figure 6: List of items to introspect upon post your Career shift decision

But for me, Rajeshwari, the corporate person, I was still grappling with the question of my own identity – whether it was writing or painting? These may be great as hobbies, but would they convert into careers? After all, I had spent 15 years in a very demanding career. There was no particular childhood talent that I had which I wanted to take forward in my adult life. It was becoming increasingly clear to me that I had to arrive at my own formula based on my own understanding, my work experience and my relationships.

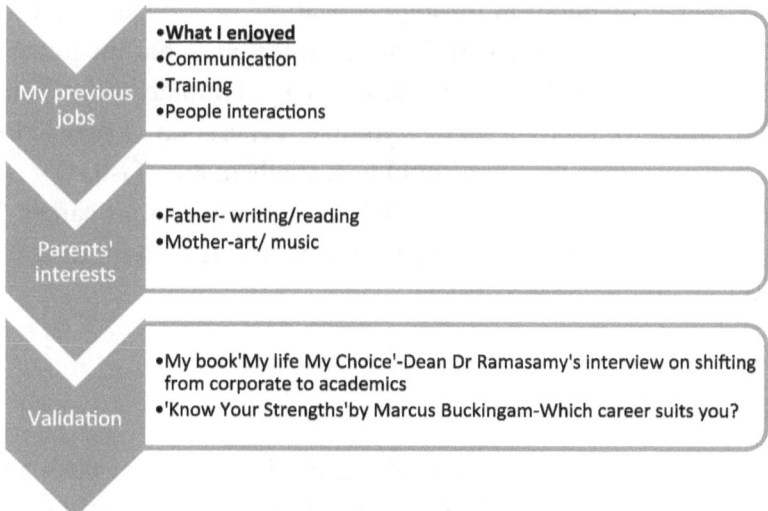

Figure 7: Details of Career shift process

It was during this time that I chanced upon a batchmate to encourage me to write a book on the subject of mid life career choices. The journey of writing the book itself was very rewarding and I became an author in the process. The book talked a lot about the various career options that one could seek after long corporate stints, such as entrepreneurship, getting back to a childhood passion, pursuing a job in the social sector, getting into politics or finally pursuing academics. While all the stories provided learnings on the triggers and barriers for a career change, the one that appealed to me most was the story of Dr Raju Ramaswamy who was the Dean of Anna University at that time.

Dr Raju Ramaswamy had spent 22 years in the railways before enrolling in a PhD programme in order to pursue academics as a career. He then went on to become a faculty member and was promoted to Dean later on. This story connected with me on many levels.

First and foremost, the context of industry to academics struck a chord with me. He had chosen a career that allowed him to take the learnings of his industry experience and build on them.

Teaching allows you to share what you have learnt before with a larger community. The job of a faculty member also includes influencing students beyond just academics and this appealed to me. It was almost like leaving a legacy to the next generation through education. Beyond all this, the sheer simplicity of his narration enabled me to understand that the journey of a good teacher is actually towards becoming a good human being. You are in a position where you have a set of a younger generation of people looking up to you. By virtue of this, one could potentially mature faster.

All these led to me choosing academics as my second career. In the subsequent chapter, I will talk to you about how I went about it, sharing all the details including the 'catalyst.'

What Geeta thinks?

There is a combination of the complex interplay of several push and pull factors in taking a mid-career break or shift. There may also be the possibility or tendency of people to be overly confident about their judgements and abilities. Let the decision to take a break not become a case of misplaced optimism.

The world we live places a premium value on labels – read fancy designations, fancy pay packets. We live in an insanely competitive and materialistic world that worships money, possessions, perfection and fame and never lets us take a step off the treadmill. In trying to contend ourselves with societal expectations about a stable life, we sometimes degenerate into robots.

Limits exist in the mind. It's so amazing to discover what you are capable of if you keep pushing your boundaries. Steve Jobs said, *"The people who are crazy enough to think they can change the world are the ones who do."*

Daniel Kahneman, the Israeli-American psychologist notable for his work on the psychology of judgement and decision-making as well as behavioural economics, said in the '70s that human beings are incapable of rational decision-making. Most of their decisions are based on impulses and biases but this enables them in taking the right decisions. Research indicates that mid life adults are more likely to make successful transitions experientially rather than analytically.

While contemplating a second career, one critical question that we need to ask ourselves is "What would you be glad you did, even if you failed?" This would provide some answers you are looking for. Another important question to ask oneself is "If money weren't an issue, what would I do?"

Just detesting your job or wanting to take time off to spend with your child or elderly parent is not an adequate blueprint for the next step, be it wanting to become an entrepreneur, joining an NGO or drifting into teaching or whatever else you wish to do.

Most of the time, we are like a square peg in a round hole. We are saddled with jobs we don't like. Our passion lies elsewhere. According to an article in TOI dated 27th August, 2017, a US-based survey of teenagers found that a 'YouTuber' figures as the top-most career choice for them.

Don't get carried away by the start-up euphoria. The media is clogged with the success stories of start-ups. Don't get fooled by the media hype and reports of million dollars funding secured overnight by start-ups. Not all is hunky dory. Sometimes the super-charged atmosphere and hype of a start-up slowly morphs into a stress-laden and toxic atmosphere.

Once your start-up takes off, if and when it does, there is some inflow of funding. Once funding comes, you realise to your dismay that you have actually become an employee all over again. Tyler Durden famously said in *Fight Club*, "*The things you own end up owning you.*"

You now need to recruit employees who may or may not share your passion and vision. You are in constant fear of key employees leaving. You begin to empathise with all your past companies where you threw attitude, picked up a quarrel and quit in a huff. Lori Greiner, the American inventor, entrepreneur, and television personality famously said, "*Entrepreneurs are willing to work 80 hours a week to avoid working 40 hours a week.*"

There was one start-up that was a dog spa with TVs screening cartoons like Scooby-Doo. I mean, really!

Or one could consider becoming a social entrepreneur… it does have a zing to it!

Perhaps become a hermit and wander in the Himalayas?

Even better, organic farming is so in now.

Or, join some reality show. It will probably give more money per week than what you could earn monthly in a job.

Better still, become a life coach or lifestyle coach or laughter coach… whatever that means!

All this sounded so much fun. Was I missing something? Start-ups sound good sometimes, but at the first glimpse of a recession or troubled times, the first casualties are the employees who are immediately handed pink slips.

We need to distinguish between a whim and a workable dream. Let's not go in pursuit of a dream that is set up for failure. The media is replete with success stories of people who waltzed into the sunset and it all sounds so exotic.

The famous writer Amish Tripathi actually never wanted to be a writer. What an irony that is! He actually aspired to be a historian but soon realised that it'd be a career filled with struggle. He pursued a career in marketing and finance and slowly veered towards a writing career, although he started out as a reluctant writer. It was a chance show on the History channel that changed the history of mythology fiction writing in India.

He was practical enough to not chuck away his job and become a full-time writer. He pursued his career during the day and doubled up as an author during the night. Even in an interview, Tripathi stated that he believed that it's always good to have a job on the side that can pay the bills. He did the same for himself too, continuing with his banking job until the royalty from his books equalled his income. Only then did he take the plunge to become a full-time writer.

Try to find that elusive passion in what you are already doing. Sometimes, pursuing the passion can turn the passion or purpose, call it by whatever name you may, into a bore and may become the proverbial albatross around the neck. A passion pursued during free time or weekends might not be as much fun or as fulfilling when done on a regular basis. Sometimes, it may just not be feasible to do something we love on a full-time basis as it may not provide us enough for our living. For example, one might be passionate about music but not a gifted singer.

Pursuing one's passion on a full-time basis is ideally suited for those who are born rich or where their passion pays reasonably well. Today, people are going in search of that elusive passion which may not even exist for them. People with passion and with middle-class moorings will anyway seek to monetise their passion so as to keep the fire burning, as passion alone doesn't pay the bills.

We crib and complain that we don't have enough time for all our hobbies. We need to relook and check whether we have cultivated one too many hobbies than necessary. Let's not forget that our salary is probably paying for our hobbies. We can't have it all at the same time. Even the great Indra Nooyi conceded that. If we can make our hobby pay for us, it's probably the ideal situation. But the need for money is an ever-growing need and the hobby slowly morphs into a job. After that, the hobby may not be as enjoyable as before.

BY THE FIFTH YEAR, JIM REALLY REGRETTED FOLLOWING HIS CHILDHOOD PASSION FOR ICE CREAM...

We have seen people staring into space with a dreamy smile on their face. One can't just throw away everything and live out of a car while roaming in the hills, especially if one is a caregiver. Isn't taking up the responsibility more meaningful than running after a mirage of passion or purpose?

One of my friends sent her daughter abroad to pursue her MS, as per her desire. After her parents spent tons of money on her MS, she threw it all mid-way to pursue her passion which was to teach scuba diving in Mauritius. I wonder when she had her eureka moment and how her parents handled this newly founded passion of hers. Yet, as long as she is able to sustain her passion and live off her earnings from it, good for her.

Several of the workshops on discovering your true calling or inner calling seem to be focused on creating discontent. It might confuse normal people into thinking that their life which comprises of holding a job, spending time with family, taking care of their parents and pursuing that odd hobby over the weekend is probably not happening enough.

If you feel that desk jobs kill creativity, find what else holds appeal for you then. If you enjoy teaching and interacting with students and being a professor is straight up your alley, then you need to get a PhD, especially if you are looking for a permanent position. For visiting and adjunct faculty, there are several corporate people and consultants moonlighting and you will face stiff competition.

NGOs or not-for-profit sectors could be looked at, but they pay just a fraction of what a corporate job would pay. You want to be your own boss? Great! But be prepared to slog it out, and make sure you have deep pockets. You will have equal and more responsibilities at half the pay. You could become the next Jack Ma if you are lucky. Unfortunately, research suggests that 90% of start-ups fall by the wayside. Setting up your shop is pretty much akin to training for a marathon. It is only for those who are in it for the long haul.

Sometimes a shortage of critical skills, especially in the IT sector, makes it viable to be a freelancer rather than work at one office. Today, people are working in a gig capacity[3] and this seems to be the way forward. As per a study by Manipal Global Education, 2017, there has been a boom of

---

[3] freelancing or working with short-term contracts as opposed to a permanent job

freelancers due to the growth of the internet and mobile phones. Apparently, at freelancers.com, one of the largest global online platforms for freelancers, the number of registered people from India is the highest at more than 20% of the total.

An alternative to the emotional rigours and upheavals of trying to navigate the corporate world is to opt out and become self-employed or start a business. According to Loscocco and Smith-Hunter (2004), "Women are becoming entrepreneurs at a more than proportionate rate compared to men."

A key reason for this is that self-employment or one's own business provides the flexibility for women to accommodate and balance both their work and home responsibilities. The additional stress that most often comes with continuous financial uncertainty is likely to outweigh the perceived advantages and positives of self-employment. If the woman taking a break and venturing into self-employment provides a secondary source of income, the stress may not be that bad.

There was this home-baker who was probably not even half as qualified as I am. Unable to achieve a work-life balance, she honed her baking skills and quit her job. She started conducting these baking classes demonstrating some exotically named dishes and charging 2–3k for a 4-hour session. At least 10–15 participants would attend these workshops.

A quick calculation indicated that she was earning 20–45k for a 4-hour session conducted at her place, at her convenience. The fees were obviously paid in cash and so was tax-free. She did a minimum of 2–3 sessions per week. I don't even want to do the math. She was probably earning much more than a professional who was slogging in a corporate from 9 to 5, 5 days a week. And all this while keeping an eye on her maid and cootchie-cooing her kids.

I also read about a lady whose talents were formidable. She was apparently a writer, singer, philanthropist, mother, wife, sister, daughter, friend, part-time activist, citizen of the country… Phew! In comparison, I was a writer of sorts, bathroom singer, philanthropist, daughter, sister, friend, wannabe activist, corporate citizen… not bad at all.

Avoid taking advice from people with vested interests. They might be harbouring a secret desire to do what you propose to do and probably do not have the guts or the circumstances to do the same. They could dissuade you and be the proverbial wet blanket.

Not all of us have the advantage of having a breakthrough... you probably need to press the pause button, not the panic button. Sometimes it's just a tide that needs to ebb and things will fall into place. We need to give it some time and not take knee-jerk decisions. Think well before quitting a job. Switching jobs may get you a salary jump that you might not get in your existing job, but if you are exhausted and can't muster up enthusiasm, nothing can save you. Add to that the daunting task of getting into a smooth working relationship with your new boss, co-workers, team... phew!

I will retire by 40 or 50 is a common statement heard these days. *I will slog till then and then enjoy my retired life* is the stuff dreams are made of. In this fast-paced, stressful world, can we be reasonably sure of surviving until the age of 40 or 50? What you really want to do, do it NOW! Seize the moment!

Decision-making is the one critical area where most fall short and are found to be lacking. Taking the right decision and timing our decision right is something we rarely do well. And that is perhaps the single most important trait we need to carefully cultivate.

By deciding to take a break, I felt I was entering a VUCA world[4]. My life was turned on its head. But I needed some intellectual heft. It was a choice, a conscious choice at that. In *Harry Potter and the Chamber of Secrets*, Dumbledore advised Harry Potter: "It is our choices Harry that show what we truly are, far more than our abilities." The choices we make ultimately define who we are and who we become. If we don't make the right choices or choices that are not thought through, we could become the leaf in the wind which gets blown around and tossed around depending on the direction the wind takes.

I liked my job, not sure if I loved it... but I loved myself more. And I wanted to invest in myself. The canvas was so vast. I knew that I was earning reasonably more than my expenses. I led a simple life, thanks to my bourgeois upbringing, though my siblings still considered me to be extravagant. In fact, I probably led a boring lifestyle as some of my male colleagues constantly jibed me about... "You don't drink, you don't smoke,

---

[4] Marked with volatility, uncertainty, complexity and ambiguity of general conditions and situations

don't eat out often, don't need to pay hefty school or college fees like us! What do you do with your money?"

One of my biggest concerns was the unforeseen medical expenses related to my father. I did not want to compromise on the quality of medical treatment, God forbid, should the need arise. I had done the good deed of taking a personal medical insurance policy in my father's name and that came in handy. I was covered on that front.

And so, sometimes you just need to take that leap of faith, leap into the unknown… and go for it. Listen to the suggestions and concerns of your immediate family and your close friends who understand your desire and will give you a no-holds-barred opinion… the rest is all noise.

We need to be aware of the impact of our decision on our loved ones. Although we might talk ourselves into believing that it doesn't matter if people don't support us, we do want our immediate family and close friends to believe in us and support and encourage us. We also want them as sounding boards when we fall or face an obstacle.

There was too much mental cacophony that I had to deal with. The more someone declares that something can't be done… is foolish… is a no-brainer, the more I have this urge to take the challenge head-on. I told the people in my inner circle and few other mature people who I knew, about my decision to take a break. When you voice your thoughts, it becomes a psychological commitment that you cannot back out from.

If you plan too much, there is a danger of getting into an "analysis paralysis" situation. There is no right time or appropriate time. Do it now. 'Just do it!' as Nike puts it. I knew I was trading my security for flexibility and passion fulfilment. A C-Suite job was glamorous but not tempting enough. The decisions you take may not exactly support the vox populi[5]. But firm self-belief, endurance and good wishes of the family will see you through.

Steve Jobs said, *"Your time is limited so don't waste it living someone else's life."* To make a successful mid life career change or break, you need not just a job-change plan or an alternate career plan, but a money-change plan too. If one has acquired a higher level of financial freedom, all sorts of exciting possibilities open up.

---

[5] Latin for 'voice of the people.' Refers to the opinion of a majority of people.

As per Maslow's hierarchy of needs, self-actualisation has been identified as the prime need of satisfaction that leads to contentment. Spiritual enlightenment, the pursuit of knowledge and a positive impact on society are cited as the prime examples of self-actualisation. For me, the pursuit of knowledge and taking a step back was what I was seeking fervently.

Midcareerbreaksaresubjecttorisks.Pleasedoathroughresearchbefore embarkingonit.

Chapter 4A

The Process of a Career Change

– by Rajee

The beginnings of my academic career

The first book that I published encouraged me towards an academic career. But the question still remained as to where I wanted to start the career change process. It was during one of my trips to the IIT, Chennai when I decided to explore the possibility of being a visiting faculty for marketing management. I met the Chair Professor there and requested him to provide me with an opportunity to teach a class on Brand Management – a field that I was familiar with.

Although I went without prior appointment, he was kind enough to give me a hearing. Upon giving him the details of my educational background and work experience, he asked me to handle one particular session as a part of the course that he was handling already. That particular class was for MBA students and it went very well. This experience became a turning point in building my confidence in my new academic career.

> **New network circles is instrumental in making a successful career change**

This was followed by me handling one complete course titled *New Product Development* for the 2nd year MBA batch. This again earned very good feedback. One of the students in my class, Mr R. Satyanarayanan, had earlier headed the marketing department in a private management school in Chennai called Chennai Business School (CBS). At the end of the class, he asked me if I would be interested in joining them. I was totally ecstatic with this offer; however, there was much thought required before I could take this deep plunge.

I was faced with the decision of becoming a permanent faculty at CBS. Several thoughts crossed my mind – was I ready for another full-time job? How would I manage my personal family time? Should I look for more options before pursuing this one and so on.

We all need financial stability in our lives, especially when we have children to raise. This adventurous move of mine into academics was all good, but I had responsibilities. I had to reach a point where I had a stable income every month.

I had taken the plunge into academics, so I had to dive deep. I couldn't just be floating around. After all, I knew there was so much one can learn as a full-time faculty. The growth prospects are immense; there is research, networking through conferences, teaching, mentoring, seminars and the list could go on. This is something a visiting professor never really becomes skilled at thanks to the time constraint and seasonality. And this excited me.

I decided to go and meet the Dean of CBS, Mr Sridhar Natarajan. He was an alumnus of IIT Kharagpur and IIM Bangalore. Similar to me, post his IIM days he had spent more than a decade in the industry before moving into academics. As I went to meet him for the first time, his informality and forthrightness struck me positively. We discussed my background and he was very curious to know how I had learnt about the opening for the Head of Department of Marketing. I mentioned the class I had taken at IIT for the PhD students and that Mr Sathya had referred me to CBS.

We got along very well from day 1. He came across as a very unconventional dean – highly popular with the students and tremendously self-motivated to get things done with a strong emphasis on action-orientedness. This last quality particularly appealed to me as that was contrary to the impression that I had carried about academicians!

The CBS selection protocol required me to go through 2 rounds of interview. Soon I was taken on board. Thus, I formally joined my second career of academics on March 3rd 2010, exactly 14 months after I had quit the corporate world.

My designation read *Head of department – Marketing, Retail and International Business* at CBS. In addition to the academic aspects, I had to contribute to the overall institution building of CBS. The job description contained the following aspects:

- Designing course curriculum for the 3 varsities – Marketing, Retail and International Business
- Drawing up the academic schedule for these students
- Liaising with guest/visiting faculty, especially for elective courses
- Teaching students their areas of their marketing specialisation (Marketing Management, Sales and Distribution, Brand Management, Public Relations, Customer Relationship Management and New Product Development)
- Helping in student placement and student mentoring
- Helping the institution build the brand of CBS through identified strategic initiatives

I was initially quite overwhelmed with the gamut of duties and responsibilities. That moment when I was given my offer letter and the entire job description was explained, I can honestly say that I could feel my initial excitement being weighed down by the baggage of responsibility.

Despite this, I fondly remember my first day at CBS. I entered the gates of CBS with mixed feelings. There was a preliminary emotion of intimidation and also a sense of challenge to prove myself again in a new career and to learn. I told myself, "You are finally a full-time professor; you are finally there!" Being referred to as a professor gives it's own high!

What did I enjoy and what did I not enjoy at CBS

My overall experience at CBS was very enriching. It was my first full-time faculty position, so obviously that made it very special. I really enjoyed sharing my industry experience and learnings with the students. I also had the privilege of conducting the inaugural launch event of their new campus at Sri City outside Chennai.

There were certain aspects of CBS that I thoroughly enjoyed, whereas there were some areas that were my least favourite.

I am a strong believer in organisational culture and the impact it has on employees. Just like corporate houses, every academic institute has its own culture. It's the culture that makes people want to come back to work each day. CBS had its own unique culture.

The environment was informal, with a lot of freedom and flexibility. It's a very employee-friendly place. In the corporate world you are lucky to get more than 2 (maybe 3) weeks off a year in addition to standard holidays. At CBS, I certainly found a more relaxed structure regarding this.

There were also professional development opportunities. I thoroughly enjoyed representing CBS at various seminars and at events held by government bodies. This was a new role compared to corporate life and I found it quite meaningful.

Student bonding – my first experience

The student bonding experience was my absolute favourite. I totally loved it. When teachers form positive bonds with students, classrooms become supportive spaces in which students can engage in academically and socially productive ways. Various research studies point to the fact that a positive student-teacher relationship is beneficial for students.

However, there are also studies that talk about the impact of student-teacher relationships on the well-being of teachers. The study postulates that those teachers who have a basic sense of relatedness with the students in their class, internalise experiences with students in representational models of relationships that guide emotional responses in daily interactions with students and changes the teacher's well-being in the long run.

My stint at CBS gave me my first experience at sharing a long-time bond with students. It made me feel associated and attached to my students, a feeling which I had not experienced before. I realised here how much influence a professor has in shaping minds and how much you can do with it. Besides imparting subject knowledge, we can also impact the emotional and social needs of our students.

Spending so much time with students made me feel young again. Building strong connections with students improved my well-being as well.

There is so much vibrancy, energy and vitality in a teaching environment. Every day is a new day with something new to teach, something new to learn.

Rabindranath Tagore once said, quite truly, *"A teacher can never really teach unless he is still learning himself. A lamp can never light another lamp unless it continues to burn its own flame. The teacher who has come to the end of his subject, who has no living traffic with his knowledge but merely repeats his lesson to his students can only load their minds. He cannot quicken them."*

Without even realising it, teachers have a strong ability to create a strong liking or disliking for the subject that they teach in the minds of students. The most boring of subjects can be made interesting by an inspired teacher. Professors have the power to truly inspire young individuals to mould their thought process and set them on the right path.

It is important to be accessible; students should feel comfortable reaching out to you. I remember students at CBS would reach out to me late at night or early in the mornings over texts and even phone calls. They start looking up to you. It becomes integral to create a bond.

Who said that only movies, TV and sports personalities have fans? We teachers have our own following. Nothing compares to the cheering that you get to hear when your name is announced at a seminar or a college function. The love, appreciation and gratitude that these students shower upon you is the best feeling in the world. You truly do feel like a star!

I still receive emails from students whom I have taught in the past. They always remember you. Knowing that people follow you and look up to you gives you a sense of responsibility; it makes you behave and act more responsively and eventually makes you a better person.

So why did I leave CBS?

It was all going fairly well at CBS; however, I was not getting enough time for my PhD thesis. Doing a PhD is fairly time consuming and it requires a lot of work and that becomes two-fold if you are pursuing it from a premier institute. Writing a dissertation requires hours and hours of research. My PhD journey is a separate journey and I will talk about that in the upcoming section.

I have to admit that though rewarding, my job profile at CBS was quite demanding. It required time and focus. As time passed by, it was becoming increasingly difficult for me to manage both my PhD and the responsibilities at CBS. The initial months were manageable as I was just starting out, but with time the workload grew. I felt I was not doing enough justice to my research thesis.

It was not only about just completing my PhD. It was actually about completing it successfully with excellence. I was at crossroads. Upon continuous deliberation with my family, friends and colleagues, I finally decided to leave CBS. It was not an easy decision.

The dean understood my plight. He was very encouraging and even told me I could come back anytime I wanted. He offered to give me visiting faculty positions in the courses that I had been teaching. CBS has a special place in my heart. It was my first full-time job as an academician. I owe a lot to CBS for giving me the confidence to transition from my corporate life to academics and for making the entire experience quite seamless.

I will now talk about pursuing my PhD journey.

Figure 8: Shifting to an Academic career

The PhD journey

Though I was consistently good at academics throughout my life, doing a PhD had never seriously crossed my mind. As mentioned earlier, it was during one of the conversations with the Chair Professor, Marketing at IIT that I considered enrolling in the PhD programme.

This decision made my family very happy, especially my parents who were not very convinced about me giving up my job. After all, I had given up a glamorous, lucrative career for the sake of my child and family. But with the decision to pursue my PhD, I felt vindicated. They probably thought I had chosen yet another challenge that befitted my career aspirations.

My father has always been a great supporter of education and I remember how proud he was when my only brother completed his PhD from the US close to 2 decades ago. Now his other child was embarking on the same journey. There was a lot of exhilaration that almost suggested that I had already completed my doctorate, and I had not even begun it!

The entry process into an IIT PhD programme is not easy. In my case, it comprised 2 steps – a written departmental exam aimed at testing your subject knowledge and a research aptitude exam aimed at testing your ability to think analytically. All these meant that I had to do some serious preparation. I had to get back to studying, possibly after 1994, i.e., after a gap of 16 years!

I cleared the 2 steps mentioned above and was shortlisted for a panel interview soon after. I was prepared adequately by some faculty members on what the process would entail. I had to be clear about my broad area of research and my motivation to do a PhD at this stage of life. There were 10 members on the panel who were from various departments. I seemed to have done a reasonably good job and was selected for a PhD at IIT Madras Department of Management studies for the term beginning August 2010.

There is a lot of literature on the internet about doing a PhD, but I can assure you that nothing ever comes close to what happens in real life. After working for 15 years in a company, there can be a potential inertia to go back to the classroom and work with MBA students. And of course, there is an enormous amount of workload in the PhD process that one has to be ready for.

On an average, one's PhD journey lasts around 5 years. In the first couple of years, one is expected to complete the coursework, i.e., attend classroom sessions on a set of subjects in your area. During this time, there is normally one doctoral committee meeting called the Zero DC which aims at assessing if you have finalised your area of research.

Post the coursework, at the end of 2 years, there is a viva voce examination. This is aimed at testing the knowledge that you have gained during the academic coursework along with the academic literature available in your area. This is the first serious evaluation point for a PhD student.

In my comprehensive viva examination, I was told that my language was more industry driven and less focused on academics. Though not surprising, it was clear to me that I had to work very hard on this area and imbibe an academic bent of mind in my manner of speech as well.

The next couple of years at IIT went in arriving at a specific research problem, discussing the research methodology, analysing the findings and getting to the conclusions. Of course, it is very iterative. There is a lot of learning, particularly in the area of research methodology that one has to newly acquire.

My research question was *What are the factors that affect the outcome of a new product in the FMCG (fast moving consumer goods) industry.* I choose this because as a practitioner I had struggled with the same question for close to 15 years. I had wished several times that someone would help me prioritise the key success factors while launching new products. This would have saved me an enormous amount of time and money. So when the time came for me to finalise my research question, it was a very obvious choice for me.

In my IIT PhD journey, the subject of statistics turned out to be my nemesis – almost, that is! I was not a good statistics student even back in college. There were other PhD students who trained me and I am very grateful to them. My research required collecting data from many FMCG companies, and once again, my industry experience was handy. In fact, my data collection became a key highlight of my PhD thesis as having access to so many companies was considered a huge advantage.

I spent several weeks and months (many late nights) doing the data analysis and making sense of it. One part of my thesis was also an in-depth case study that required networking with CavinKare Pvt. Ltd., a leading FMCG player where I had worked for 3 years. I completed the case study in a year's time with the encouragement and support of the entire management.

At the end of the fourth year, I was ready to start writing the final thesis report. Throughout the process, my supervisor consistently played many different roles in providing me with thought clarity, guiding me when required, encouraging me at times and of course discussing several other topics that provided a sense of relief to the otherwise monotonous PhD journey. There were also other review meetings during this 4-year period – one doctoral committee meeting to assess my progress and 2 departmental seminars where I could share my work with PhD scholars across IIT and get feedback.

The 4-year period ends in a synopsis meeting wherein the first draft of the final thesis is ready and the formal presentation is made to the Dean of Academic Research for the first time. By this time, external viewers who will examine the work will have been identified. The draft may undergo some changes post the synopsis meeting and the final copies are sent to the reviewers for examination (these reviewers are kept confidential by the institute).

Defence viva

After many moments of uncertainty, you reach a point when you sometimes question yourself on whether you took the right decision to even start a PhD journey. But the defence viva step enables you to have hope that you will actually finish your PhD thesis. The viva clearance itself maybe a speculative process and there are several reasons for this. The first could be that there is no one formula to get this right. Right from the time we finish our submission of the revised comments by the reviewers, we are just waiting for the D date, i.e., defence viva date.

The waiting time mostly comprises of people advising you on what to expect in the viva. While there may be several inputs, the people who will have the maximum relevance in the process are the supervisor, the doctoral committee and your peers. In fact, you could do a dry run of the defence process with your peers and get them to ask questions about your thesis. I did that. Ensure you record them and try to answer each of them later. By the time you get to the actual viva, you should feel comfortable with the range of questions that may be thrown at you.

The duration of the actual defence viva could be between 30 minutes to a couple of hours. Typically, both the reviewers may attend, both domestic and international. If the latter is not available, then a representative from the department from where you are graduating will attend. He or she would have been given the examiner's questions earlier. Post the successful completion of the viva, you leave as Dr ... and this is indeed a very rewarding moment.

Deciding to do a PhD is a function of many factors – especially around one's middle age. At this time, there are many stakeholders in one's life and their commitment is equally important to taking that time off from a regular paying job. Also, their motivation will help you clear all those daunting exams that are in store in a PhD process. The long hours in a classroom (with other students far younger), away from home or office, can be quite an experience! Overall, do it only if you are embarking on a career based on it as the efforts are quite substantial.

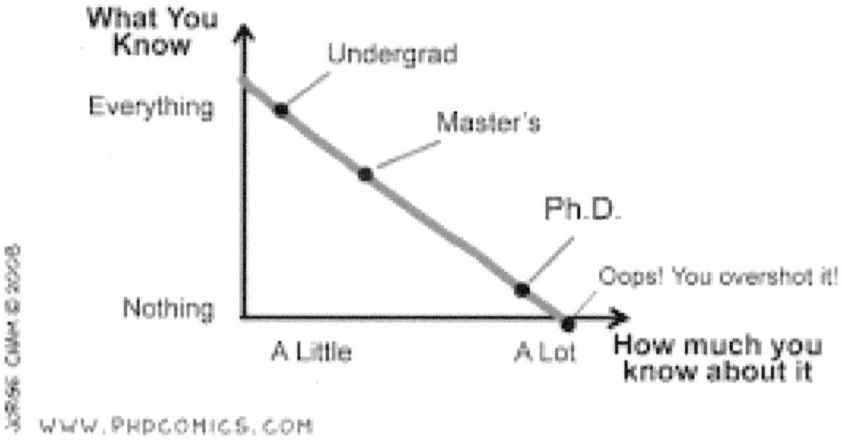

Figure 9: What you know vs How much you know about it

Visiting faculty at other IIMs

When you do your PhD from a premier institute like IIT, your visibility goes up. There are faculty members from other esteemed institutes who visit IIT and you get a chance to meet and interact with them. Your supervisor may also introduce you to them and talk to them about your credentials. Thus, your chances of getting a visiting faculty assignment at other IIMs/IITs go up. It happened to me as my supervisor was familiar with the director of one of the IIMs and I eventually was introduced to him.

When I received a call for a visiting faculty assignment from an IIM, my happiness knew no bounds. I was quite elated to hear the news that I was getting an opportunity to teach at my alma mater. It felt incredible, yet my feeling of excitement was soon replaced by anxiety and nervousness.

After all, I had graduated more than 16 years earlier and a feeling of self-doubt started creeping in. "Will I be underprepared? Am I good enough for this role?"

Which places to visit and why?

So how does this whole thing of handling a visiting faculty assignment work and how do you be a success at it?

First and foremost is choosing the right institutes to visit. I started off with my list of institutes to apply. Having various friends in academia helped to give some direction at this stage.

Being an alumni from an IIM myself, what could be a better place than that to start my search? I looked up the websites of various IIMs and found that IIM Ranchi had advertised for visiting faculty at that time. I wrote to the director, scheduled an appointment with him and met him. I must mention that the responsiveness of the directors at the various IIMs is something remarkable – they almost always reply to emails (I have heard this from many people).

I was called for an interview process that was a combination of a research seminar, a classroom teaching session and a personal interview. The first is aimed at gauging how good one is in terms of research abilities and the objective of the teaching session is to test whether one is good at communicating with students in a classroom setting. Since I had already been teaching at various places (IIT, CBS), IIM Ranchi decided to waive off the second step.

This was my first research seminar and I was not even halfway through my PhD journey, so naturally I was a bit jittery. I chose a topic within the purview of my PhD: *New Product Development Success Factors*. The seminar was attended by the faculty of IIM Ranchi and the director himself. There were also faculty members from the marketing area from other IIMs.

As I made my presentation, I realised that there were some areas that I definitely needed to improve upon, especially the academic language, i.e., I was still using a lot of corporate industry terminology that is not particularly welcomed in an academic institution. Overall, it went ok and I was called for the personal interview. I was asked questions on the various theoretical concepts of what I was teaching. I had to definitely brush up on the concepts. Fortunately, I had read up on the latest textbooks on marketing management. It is especially important to have theoretical knowledge of the course that one wants to teach.

Here, I want to emphasise a point to people with industry experience. Many just assume that they can join academia simply based on their work experience. This is not completely true. Though one may have had long stints in the industry, it is still very important to establish the fact that you are capable of research and teaching students. Not all who have knowledge become good teachers. Teaching is a skill by itself. It goes beyond simply recalling anecdotal evidence of what works and what doesn't. One needs to be prepared to answer questions, be challenged by students and be interested in building relationships with them beyond the classroom.

Added to all this is the administrative work involved as a full-time faculty. You will need to set question papers, correct answer sheets and be ready to do institution building activities such as placements or industry interface and so on. In essence, corporate experience may be a stepping stone into academia, but it does not guarantee that you will make a good academician.

In this case, I did get selected as a faculty at IIM Ranchi and was given a provisional letter to join them full-time once I complete my PhD. Meanwhile, I could continue as visiting faculty. I was happy as I liked the tag of being called a faculty member of an IIM!

The other institutes that I applied to and taught at as visiting faculty were IIM Indore, IFMR, Great Lakes and IIT Madras. All these are premier institutes and I knew that if I taught as a visiting faculty in these, finding a permanent position would be easier.

My thoughts on the subject of visiting faculty assignments:

Choosing the right institute

Choose the very best institutes when you start out. The credibility that it adds to your profile is unparalleled. Even if you have landed a visiting faculty position at a Tier 2 B-School at a very good pay, my suggestion is to try for Tier 1 institutes. Half your job is done when your CV shows teaching experience from these institutes, and of course, there is so much that you get to learn which in due course makes you job market ready. I am not saying you would not land a full-time faculty position if you taught at Tier 2 B-Schools, but being a visiting faculty at Tier 1 B-Schools just adds that extra bit of credibility.

How do you gain access?

To obtain the position of a visiting faculty is not as easy as it may sound. Simply applying for the position is not enough. This is the era of referrals and it's no different even in the case of this role. The institute should be convinced that the visiting faculty is of a certain stature and is bringing in knowledge that would benefit the institute.

Teaching before research

At this point, the focus should be on teaching. The interview panel will require you to be specific about your experience in teaching in certain areas. These areas should be original and memorable. Giving examples within a particular domain of say marketing (such as *can we focus on Facebook marketing or Ambience marketing?*) will build interest and relevance and your application will stand out.

Research is also important

If you have done past research work, it will also figure prominently in this deliberation. So highlight at least some publications (you should have started work or fully published some by now – if not in international journals, at least in others). Also outline a future research agenda that you will have regarding how will take your PhD thesis forward once you finish it.

I can't agree more with Karen Kelsky, a career consultant, who runs the website "The Professor Is In." She rightly says in the article *How Do I Pitch Myself for a Visiting Assistant Professorship*, "You need to show familiarity with – and interest in – the department, its faculty, its students and its programme initiatives and curricula. While it's true you are only there for a year, you are nevertheless probably competing for this position against hundreds of other candidates."

How do you gain acceptance?

Having a flourishing career as a visiting faculty requires you to keep getting assignments from various institutes. It's not enough to get just 1 or 2 assignments; sustainability is the key. This will only happen when an institute is assured of the faculty's credibility and has something to gain in return.

From my experience, I can surely say that having an outstanding teaching record is pivotal to gaining acceptance.

Teaching experience is a necessary condition but definitely not a sufficient condition to land a job. There are other factors which are very influential in gaining a faculty position. This includes research, publication record, networking and personal contacts. As I have already mentioned previously, contacts are important in the academic world. By no means am I trying to say that just by having contacts you can have a flourishing career as an academician. Contacts may help you land a job, but you indisputably need the talent to survive.

I am aware that many people find the idea of networking very daunting. I belonged to this school of thought as well, but over the years, I changed and realised that networking is simply about taking an interest in others and developing a relationship with those that share your passion and interests.

So how do you network? Start with asking other people questions about their work and career, basically taking the focus off you and make them the centre of attention. You could try keeping in touch with people you meet at various conferences and seminars. These encounters may be the beginning of a mutually beneficial relationship. Not every person you connect with will bring in business. It is a process and it takes time, but you need to start doing it. With time, you never know you might become a natural at it.

Benefits of being a visiting faculty

Being a visiting faculty has its perks. There is no long-term commitment or obligation which you need to serve and that leaves you with much freedom and independence. There is desirable flexibility in terms of schedule. So basically, you can dictate your working hours. This was a saving grace for me because that is what had made me take the plunge from corporate to academia – the need for personal time.

The downside of being a visiting faculty

I do not want to paint just a beautiful picture of what it is to be a visiting faculty. There are quite a few stumbling blocks. Not having a long-term commitment to an Institute may appear advantageous in the short run. However it also has another side to it; your focus at work might tend to drop. One has to keep motivating oneself, otherwise there are chances of slacking off.

I have always loved interacting and building good relationships with students. Teaching as a visiting faculty doesn't give you enough time to build a long-term relationship with students. I personally despised this most during my stint as a visiting faculty.

Most people are of the opinion that visiting professors get paid less. Well, it is not written in stone. It purely depends on many factors: institute budgets, expertise or star power of the visiting faculty, duration of the visit, etc. It is advisable to get acquainted with the pay scales in your discipline and your university of choice. Seasonality in cash flow is definitely a negative aspect, especially when you have a family to support and you are the only earning member.

In addition, a visiting faculty position is devoid of certain privileges that a full-time faculty member enjoys. You may not be able to do any research work under the institute name, you may not be considered for any new plum courses that are introduced at the institute and you may be not be given priority over permanent faculty when classes are being scheduled.

It is important to clarify in advance what you will be expected to do during your time as a visiting faculty. This will lay the rules of the game and make sure you are clear about what the university has to offer.

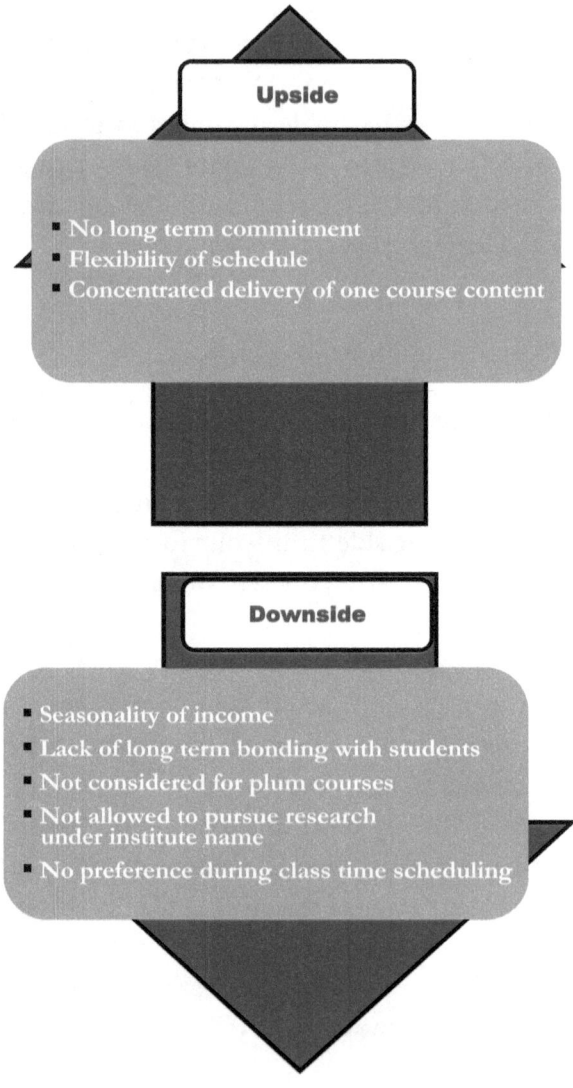

Figure 10: The two sides of being a visiting faculty

Visiting faculty – Course outline

The most critical thing while you apply for a visiting faculty position is to prepare your course outline, and quite honestly, it's the toughest part. The course outline has to be designed by you perfectly and it should get accepted.

My suggestion is to look at course outlines of similar subjects from different institutes. That's a good starting point and you can build up from there. A word of caution: please look carefully through the other courses taught and their outlines to avoid any sort of duplication. I remember working halfway through my course outline and then realising there was a similar subject being taught at the university and there was severe duplication.

Building the course outline gives you an opportunity to see how content from other courses relates to your own – is my content redundant or reinforcing? Am I teaching my content at the right level?

Course outline

Developing this is not easy. First, I would advise you to choose a course title that falls within the courses offered by that institute in that area. For example, if it is marketing, look at the institute's website and draw up a list that may be within your purview. This should be followed by talking to faculty members in that area to see what's new. You could even look at outlines offered on the internet to get an idea. Pick the key textbooks and go through them to educate yourself on the various concepts.

These steps will also give you a comprehensive view. There are many resource materials these days, starting with videos, PowerPoint presentations, quizzes, etc. The key is to first understand and list out various aspects of the course you are offering. What are contemporary and which are the ones that you can do justice to.

Once this list is in place, start reading up on the latest articles from Google Scholar or other databases that represent the work in that area. You can also select a business case for discussion. If your institute subscribes to electronic databases, you can look up Harvard Business School (HBS),

Emerald and so on. Put in a video if you think that would liven up the discussion. Finally, you may want to include some group work or a field project. The last one adds value in terms of experiential learning for the students.

The outline approval process varies across different B-Schools, but the common part is that it is put up for discussion amongst the specific area or domain (Marketing, Finance, etc.). Usually it is anonymous in order to ensure the objectivity of comments. The feedback is gathered and sent back to the concerned faculty for making changes. Post this, a round of approval is sought and if that is cleared, then the outline is approved. The overall process can take anywhere between 3–6 months depending on the type of course, its newness and the immediacy of it being offered.

Some places like IIM-B provide the opportunity to the faculty to send a video clip 'selling' the course to the students before their enrolment. They believe that the students should get a chance to hear from the concerned faculty on whether this course will add value and how. Also in some other places such as XLRI, there is a discussion forum with the students on how this course fits into other courses and how students can benefit from this. All these elements increase the likelihood of the course being accepted.

Even if the course is rejected, it is useful to get feedback on why this happened. This will help the faculty member prepare better the next time.

Developing and getting the course outline approved is probably the most important step in one's academic career – over a period of time, as you get used to teaching a particular course and earning a name for yourself in that, the process becomes easier to get into a particular institute. Constant improvisations are required to keep up with the incoming batch of students but the value addition becomes easier as you gain more experience.

Please refer to Appendix 2 for a sample course outline.

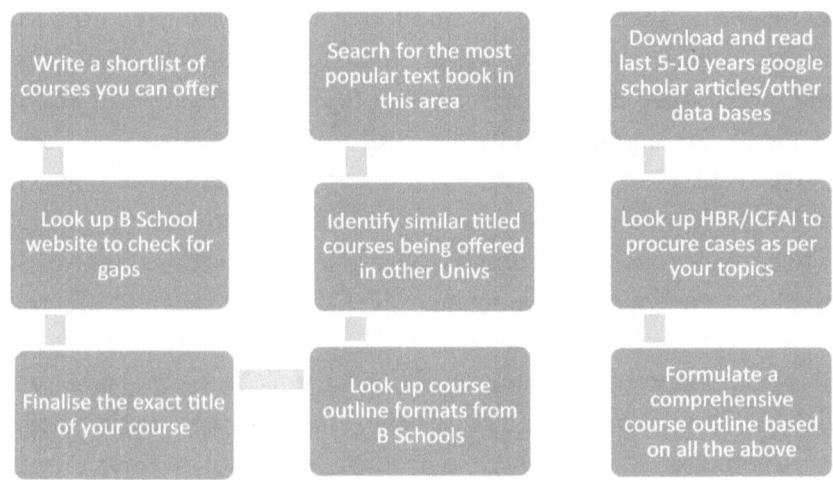

Figure 11: Developing a course outline for a B-School

XLRI – A big milestone in my academic career

While CBS was my first full-time job in my academic career, XLRI was the first one that I got after I completed my PhD. This was significant as XLRI has ranked amongst the top 3 institutes in the country over the past decade. It is also an institute that highly values the corporate experience of a faculty member while still encouraging research. XLRI was ideal for a person with my background.

I had met a senior professor in marketing during my IIM Ranchi visits earlier on and he had had egged me to apply. So when I went for the interview selection process, I was comfortable. I met many other eminent faculty members who were stars in their own right, and the start to my academic journey was impeccable.

What do I say about XLRI? The campus is just right with a combination of nature, up-to-date infrastructure, regular events, lovely weather, amazing management – all good things combined. In the marketing area, I had a combination of corporate experience as well as my PhD from IIT, so it all worked well.

The selection process was again a combination of a research seminar and teaching a class. (The latter was waived for me due to my prior teaching experience) When I prepared for the research seminar at XLRI, I found it useful to look at their website and understand what the need gaps in that area were. This is evident from research areas of faculty members that are listed. Once I knew this, I prepared on a topic for presentation as per my interest area and aligned with the existing area head. Remember, normally institutes recruit only based on their needs. There is also a one-on-one interview process that follows where you meet the dean and the director.

The way the faculty selection happens at a premier educational institute is based on an overall discussion amongst the faculty members. Hence the faculty's behaviour at the research seminar, her ability to handle questions calmly/thoroughly and the buy-in from various team members are all important. They also look for consensus from all other faculty members while selecting a new member, so it is important to present a seminar amiably to be able to appeal to all. This is a key difference between the selection process between a corporate and an academic job.

Choosing an academic career

Having said all of this, choosing an academic career is not easy. The phrase *the grass is always greener on the other side* was apt for my situation. There is always an initial hesitation period, followed by analysis, some trial and then decision-making.

And here I was with a big decision to make. The major reason behind leaving my corporate career was to have some personal time with family and now I had landed in a situation where I needed to settle down in a different city, which meant being away from family. Did I really want to do this?

My mind was flooded with thoughts. *Joining XLRI, is this the right thing to do! It will surely give a massive boost to my academic career, but what about my family time? What about my personal commitments?*

A couple of days passed by and my mind was a myriad of thoughts. I received a call from my dad who suggested that such decisions cannot be made just by yourself and there are certain important factors to consider before reaching a decision. This call from my dad definitely helped calm my nerves and I knew what needed to be done.

Involvement of stakeholders in decision-making

One thing was very clear to me; this could not be my decision alone. I needed consent from the people who would be impacted by my decision to choose my academic career, which obviously involved my family.

My father was very optimistic about XLRI. He was thrilled with the whole idea of me being a professor at XLRI. Then came the toughest part, involving my son in this decision-making. I didn't want to force this decision down his throat. On our drive back from his school, I narrated my situation stating it as a challenge that one of my friends was facing.

My son at once understood that I was narrating my own dilemma to him and replied with a smile saying that I didn't have to do this and that he would give his honest opinion on the subject. He said "Mom, you can do whatever makes you happy. I am sure you can manage both home and work."

Could I, really? Sitting 775 miles away from Chennai, would I be able to monitor my household; would it affect my child's upbringing? There were so many questions. I had got encouraging responses from my family. They would certainly stand by my decision. Yet the final decision was mine, and there was a lot of soul searching to do.

Mid life career changing decisions are not easy, and it becomes even more difficult if you have to choose between your career and your personal time.

Spending time at home

How important is it to spend time at home and more importantly how much time? Nature has blessed women with the ability to multitask. The new age woman is juggling many roles more efficiently than before. Whether one chooses to work or be a homemaker, both are equally important despite their different roles. The key lies in striking a balance between work and home.

Making time for kids and one's spouse is crucial for a fulfilling married life. It has been revealed by various studies that men spend more time than women doing paid work while women spend more time than men on household work and childcare. About 33% of parents feel that they do not have enough time with their kids. I did not want to have a sense of regret for not spending enough time at home. However, I also passionately wanted to pursue my career and I knew not doing so would be detrimental to my emotional well-being. After all, when we are not happy, we cannot do real justice with what we have to offer to our loved ones.

There is a very interesting study done by the University of Maryland which found that the pressure to spend so much quality time with children stresses mothers out so much that it may actually make us worse parents than if we focused more time on making more money and less on frontal lobe development and building a deep connection with our kids. It doesn't really matter how much time you spend with your children; what matters is how you spend your time with them.

A study like this is very important in lifting the guilt off the chest of working moms and educating us on what is good for both mothers and children. Also, another study reveals that divorce rates are lesser in marriages where both the partners are happily employed.

Evaluation of individuals

There are no said rules in life; in fact, there are no said theories that apply to everyone. We all react differently to stimuli. Just because a certain Mrs X was able to balance her family and career perfectly, it doesn't imply that I will be a success at this decision too. It is extremely crucial to evaluate oneself while making such decisions. I needed to evaluate myself, my strengths, my weaknesses. How much do I really know myself?

Most people don't know themselves as well as they think. I turned to past events to get a clearer picture of myself. My previous career in marketing involved a lot of travel, so there had been various episodes of me being away from home and it wasn't that hard. But this time it was different. I was required to be stationed in a different city and make occasional visits to my family, my home. How tough would this be? The mother in me answered, "Very tough to say the least."

My son was very comfortable and happy staying with the house help that we had. She had been with us since his birth and was dependable. I knew that my son and husband would manage well without me being there, but was it enough? What about the bonding time with my son? How about my time with my ageing parents? How much could I cover up during these occasional visits? What about my focus at work? Would I be able to focus at work or would my mind worry about my family's well-being?

These were questions I needed to answer for myself and that required self-evaluation, knowing what I could and could not do. As time went by, I quickly realised that it would be a trade-off; I couldn't have it all, and some sacrifices had to be made. Which option would relatively hurt less was the question at hand.

> **Changes are uncomfortable, but most often than not something good comes out of it**

After much analysis, I knew what I wanted. The solution was clear; impeccable balance between my career and home. I had to do it, even though it would be tough. It would involve a lot of hard work from my side, including frequent travel between Jamshedpur and Chennai but I believed that I had what it takes. I was ready for it.

Short-term vs Long-term

I had decided to accept the offer from XLRI. I felt a sense of relief about accomplishing the much difficult task of taking a decision. Reaching a conclusion was one of the hardest choices I've had to make.

The next step was to inform my son and parents. My son took it quite well and said "Why should I worry? You are just a phone call away." My happiness knew no leaps and bounds with the supportive behaviour of my family until I went and met my father.

My father has always been my best critic. He knew that there had been times in the past when I had been hasty with my decisions. Smiling wryly over a cup of coffee he said, "Rajeshwari, a decision is a good decision only if it is sustainable. I want you to tell me how long can you do this."

I knew I was ready for a start at XLRI, but I had not given a lot of thought into whether I would be able to sustain it for a long time. When we make career choices, it is integral that a considerable amount of thought has been put into the sustainability of the decision.

The woman who went to meet her father was confident and happy and full of excitement, but the same woman on her way back was all muddled – a piece of the puzzle was still missing. The meeting with my father had given me enough food for thought for the next few days. There were only a couple of days left for me to communicate my decision and sign the offer letter.

Would I be able to juggle my career and family life well and for how long? If a woman does continue on her career path, she needs to be a logistical genius. She needs to organise childcare and oversee impossible schedules. In a survey conducted on Harvard MBAs, it was indicated that what they aimed for and continued to value was both a fulfilling professional and personal life. However, their ability to realise them according to gender had played out very differently over time.

Men were more likely to be in senior management positions than women. The survey also showed that women were less satisfied with their careers and found that 77% of HBS graduates overall – 73% of men and 85% of women – believed that 'prioritising family over work' is the number one barrier to women's career advancement. Also, most men expected their career to take precedence and the woman's career to take a back seat.

I knew that I needed this experience from XLRI to give my academic career a big push and after much pondering, I believed that the decision would be long-term. Like they say "You won't know it till you don't do it." I had to take the risk.

Thoughts after getting there

The decision was made, the offer letter signed and communicated. It was time to take the plunge. I still vividly remember the moment when it was time for my family to leave after dropping me. I stood at the gates of XLRI like a child on her first day to school who was waving to her parents all teary-eyed after being dropped off at school. The first 2 weeks felt like years.

To everyone who asked me how I was doing, I would say, "very well" cheerfully yet with a little sadness in my heart. I had stayed away from family on various occasions before but somehow it seemed more painful now. During my corporate career, each time I would travel for work I knew that it was only a matter of days and I would be back soon and that was enough to comfort me. But this was different.

However, within a month, things changed. I became increasingly comfortable with my new workplace and in my new home away from home. I loved my job. XLRI gave me immense opportunities to further enhance my skillset. Living on campus provided the much-needed focus for pursuing my research agenda. The peer group faculty was of a very high intellectual calibre and were very warm. This ensured my comfort away from family.

Having come with industry experience from places like HUL and CavinKare, XLRI showcased my strengths perfectly. I obtained consistently good teaching feedback scores and this motivated me immensely. Overall, at a professional level, I had found my match in XLRI and it set my career on a new trajectory.

On a personal level, my time at XLRI was equally enjoyable. One of the concerns you have when you change jobs and your location in your forties is whether you will find yourself social moorings in the new area. XLRI's Management Development Programme (MDP) guesthouse did the trick for me. The friends that I acquired here were soon to become lifelong ones.

Other faculty members were staying in that place and we all hit it off very well. In addition to discussing matters with regard to academics, our lunch/dinner conversations were about books, movies, research topics, conferences, etc. All these made me feel at home. There were also frequent drives that we undertook as the 'MDP Gang' which were educative and entertaining. All in all, I was rapidly falling in love with XLRI, the B-School as well as the people there!

Within my first 6 months at XLRI, I was quite sure that I had made the right choice. I had a very productive first year with 3 research publications, some management development programmes and great teaching scores. In fact, I had completed the task of converting my PhD thesis into a B-School usable textbook during that year! But I did miss home terribly and I frequently worried about the well-being of my family members. Every opportunity that I got, I would make a visit back home. I was always conscious though that it was my decision to join XLRI and I had to stick to it; there were sacrifices but there were also rewards, and I chose to focus on the rewards.

For a woman, choosing career over personal time comes at some cost. But the sense of fulfilment is inexplicable. My experience at XLRI was indeed rewarding to say the least. But could it make up for the lost time with my family back home? This is one question I still don't have an answer to.

As I talk to many women and men on this topic of an academic career, one thought that comes through consistently is whether an academic career suits a woman better than it suits a man? Let us evaluate this in the next chapter.

Chapter 4B

Back to School

– by Geeta

"Have the courage to follow your heart and intuition. They somehow know what you truly want to become."

– Steve Jobs

Why PhD?

Like several people who make the switch from corporate to academics, I too dabbled with this thought during my corporate stint. There was no particular defining moment or *aha* moment for me to decide on getting my PhD. I had harboured this desire since I was in school, when it dawned on me that my father is a PhD and a postdoc to top it.

Friends and family would look at him with awe and that aura around him filled me up with this burning desire to do my PhD at some point in my life. Having been anointed an academic ninja by my peers, a PhD seemed like the logical conclusion – the proverbial icing on the cake. Not to forget that a PhD is the highest level of an academic degree one can pursue and obtain in India and most other nations.

Chennai was like an alma mater. Given that I was taking care of my ageing father, I needed to keep his convenience in mind before taking any decision to pursue my PhD outside Chennai. When I realised that he was most comfortable at Chennai, I didn't have the heart to relocate him. So Chennai became my bailiwick.

I decided to pursue my PhD from IIT which I felt was the best place in Chennai for that. I could have chosen to do my PhD from the local university which might have not been as rigorous. But then, with my lofty ambitions, I aspired to do it at one of the top universities.

I questioned myself on my life's direction. I had faced success and setbacks during my corporate tenure. I may not have been the 'super-successful' corporate honcho that I could have been, but I prided myself on living life on my terms.

Doing my PhD was like a long call option in my life. The downside risk was to not complete it, coupled with the huge opportunity loss of income. The potential upside and the payoff though were infinite according to me. For me, achieving my doctorate had become my holy grail. One needs to have a strong *fingerspitzengefühl*, (borrowing from German, don't bother looking it up) to embark on this journey. I was neither breaking bad nor trying to prove a point to someone.

I was looking forward to being pleasantly surprised by my journey.

Cracking the code

> *"To be yourself in a world that is constantly trying to make you something else is the greatest accomplishment."*
>
> – Ralph Waldo Emerson.

I applied to the Department of Management Studies (DOMS) at IIT with my grade sheets and certificates. The first round of shortlisting is normally based on one's academic credentials. So, I felt almost certain that I would get a call. I didn't. My pride was badly hurt. I wanted to know the reason and I went in person to the office to investigate.

I was told very matter-of-factly that I had not secured 70% in my Chartered Accountancy (CA) exam and, hence, was not shortlisted. For the love of God! I realised that 70% was the cut-off that was uniformly applied to all the postgraduate courses. Basically, similar cut-off marks were being applied for engineering students and CAs. I had to then patiently explain to them about the rigours to pass the CA course and the marks generally secured by the rankers and narrate tales of abysmally low pass percentage and so on. I hope you get the drift. I had anyway missed the bus by then. So I reapplied again 6 months later and finally got a call. Yo!

As luck would have it, November 18 was fixed as the date for the test and interview and I was to leave for my cousin's wedding on the 12th and I had planned to get back by the 16th. I nevertheless prepared whatever I could. It was a unique experience to get back to books after so many years. I had to appear for an exam, which was mandatory for those applicants who had completed their last degree more than 10 years prior. There were 3 of us who appeared for the exam.

The exam basically tested my concepts in finance, aptitude, etc. The exam done, I was whisked away to the interview room where a panel comprising of professors from the finance department interviewed me. I had prepared a draft proposal on the research area of my interest, which was scanned by the panel. I was quizzed on a number of factors. Their main concern was whether I would be able to cope with the rigours demanded of a PhD.

They basically wanted to know if I was just infatuated with the idea of doing a PhD. They wanted to know if I would be able to survive without the fat corporate paycheque. I then expressed my desire to undertake my PhD on a part-time basis, which was met with instant disapproval. I was told point blank that part-time PhD was not encouraged in finance as they had a bad experience in the past where part-time researchers took their own sweet time to complete their research. I tried to reason with them but was vetoed. I finally gave my nod for a full-time PhD. It was a Hobson's choice anyway.

I was not an MBA, mind you, and the course was focused more on finance than accounts and taxation. I waited with bated breath and by mid-day, I was told I had been shortlisted for the final round. So far so good. Another interview followed. This time it was with a cross-functional panel of about 7 senior professors. Post the second interview, I left after being told that the results would be communicated in a couple of days. I didn't hear from them even after a week, so I gave up the idea, thinking it was just not meant to be.

Nevertheless, I decided to call and find out the probable reasons for not getting admitted. I was coolly told by the office desk that I was very much selected and a mail had been sent to me in this regard. Wow! I found out that one of the most important mails of my life had landed in my spam box. I was elated and punched the air.

Convincing stakeholders

It was only later that I broke the news to my family. My father looked both proud and worried. Dittoo with my sisters. My father, being a first generation PhD in the family, was happy that his daughter would carry the mantle and become the second generation PhD. But they were worried about my ability to physically cope with the rigours and about my financial strength to see me through.

I boasted to them that I was a finance person and could manage to tide over without major hassles. Actually, I was not quite sure of it myself but nevertheless had to assuage their feelings. Middle-class concerns of throwing away the security of a job and not having a steady flow of income for 3, maybe 4, 5 or God knows how many years, can easily rattle anyone. It was imperative for me to get a buy-in from my family, especially my father. My generation is probably the last of the generations which still place a lot of importance on their parents' wishes and advice. *The veneration generation*, as I call my generation.

Some colleagues looked at me with melancholic scepticism. Few relatives and friends were flummoxed with my decision. They openly indulged in unwarranted ultracrepidarianism. A variety of opinions where shared:

> *Why would you want to study at this age?*
> *What's wrong with you? Just relax, you are in a decent job and getting a decent salary.*
> *Are you off your rocker?*

Why are you doing this to your father at this age? Read 'the guilt factor.'
You are committing professional hara-kiri.
Do you think you are going to change the world with your PhD?
Is a PhD really useful?
You will loose momentum in your corporate career and will need to start from scratch should you join academics after your PhD...

I realised it would be very difficult for people to comprehend my esoteric desire. I was trending *#geetahaslosthermind* in my circle. For all the naysayers, I wanted to borrow a leaf out of *Gone with the Wind* and say, "Frankly my dear, I don't give a damn." Although some concerns were genuine, I nevertheless decided to pursue my desire in the face of all obstacles. It was after all my ultimate desire.

To paraphrase Charles Dickens, "It was the best of times, it was the worst of times. It was the epoch of my belief, it was the epoch of others' incredulity."

Life at IIT

The first day when I walked into the IIT campus, not as a wanderer or a lollygagger but as a researcher, my heart swelled with pride. The campus is a veritable Shangri-La in the midst of the hustle and bustle of the overcrowded city. The long unwinding levelled roads, the greenery in particular, the deer crossing the road with gay abandon, no traffic, no pollution... it was so beautiful. It was a mini city within the city. I just loved it. Just entering the campus seemed to soothe me and fill me with a sense of pride.

Choosing a guide

The issue now was of identifying a guide who worked in the same field as that of my area of interest. The guide also had to agree to take me under her wings. Some guides were not in favour of a 'senior' student. They had their concerns about the seriousness of such students and their ability to withstand the pressures that research demanded. Choosing a guide is the most critical factor for the successful outcome and timely completion of your thesis. The guide will have the final say in approving and allowing a student to submit her thesis. One needs to ensure that your guide is equally passionate and well-versed in the topic you choose for your research.

Working under a tenured professor has its advantages. Firstly, since tenure guarantees employment, they are more stable and secure and are not stressed and grappling with their own insecurities. Faced with innumerable obstacles, lack of funds, opposition, critical reviews from peers/experts and umpteen paper rejections, the only thing that keeps you going is the deep-rooted passion and unshakeable conviction in your research, apart from some solid guide support.

After the finalisation of my guide, I met her and my co-researchers who had registered with the same guide. They were almost half my age and looked so relaxed and confident. Was I a tad late and too old to be doing my PhD? I was the latest satellite, 3rd to be precise, to be added to my guide.

There were just a couple of women in my age group pursuing their PhD in other disciplines. One of them told me point-blank that I had probably made the biggest mistake of my life by quitting my job to do a PhD on a full-time basis. I was taken aback but chose to ignore the comment.

It was a new experience to be surrounded by toppers from different fields. It was a great leveller. I had to unlearn several things in order to fit in. When I made presentations, I was told that it was too 'corporatish' and I should abide by the diktats of the academic institutions and mould myself. I would hear this refrain constantly through my stint. I guess I was suffering from the lag effects of my corporate stint. I now observed others and shaped my presentation style to suit the academic requirements.

Penny-pinching my way through my PhD

I suddenly felt like a bootstrapped start-up myself. I had not written the MAT or any other qualifying exam. Hence, I was not entitled to any scholarship or stipend. Although it was then a meagre 8k–10k, it was at least some money to meet basic needs. But on the flip side, it entailed taking up some duties in the library, invigilation, guide-related work and so on. I somehow didn't fancy myself doing these odd jobs and hence refrained from taking the exam, despite some colleagues advising me to take it. I sat on my high horse and proclaimed that I wouldn't be seen doing these 'menial' jobs.

The first year ensured that I was well-dressed given my expensive corporate wardrobe that I displayed in full glory. That year I received more compliments for my outfits and accessories than my academic accomplishments. By the end of the second year, I was in my faded glory.

My sister and friends started gifting me dresses and bags for my birthday. Then they started gifting me dresses for festivals, star birthday, completing my comprehensive viva, scoring an S and then just simply. Never mind if some of the dresses were lurid green or vomit yellow in colour. A look at my wardrobe revealed several outfits that had not been worn, some waiting to be stitched for several weeks, sometimes months, some faded and worn out but being kept for purely sentimental reasons. I rearranged and soon had a functional wardrobe with clothes that I could wear. Clothes were not discarded immediately on the first sign of fading. On few occasions, the maid actually appeared to be better dressed than I.

I was bordering on becoming a minimalist. A friend who was a hotshot in this huge corporate world and whose mobile bills were on the house, told me to give him a missed call whenever I wanted to speak to him. "Don't waste your money," he said like a wise old lady. I very cheaply agreed to the proposition.

In order to generate some income, I relied on my teaching skills and coached some CA/CIMA aspirants and earned some money. While there were several requests for coaching, I handpicked the few who were sincere and committed. Some parents would come opinion shopping. We live in a strange place where people don't flinch or bat an eyelid when beauty parlours raise their service rates arbitrarily. But they negotiate on something as fundamental as education.

Some friends requested that I offer some odd advisory services to their clients. I survived the first year. By the end of the first year, my guide (God bless her!), in a bid to ease my monetary pressure, had applied and obtained a grant from the CA institute which was related to my area of work. It ensured some stipend for 18 months. This however continued for a period of 10 months only and we had to pre-close the assignment.

This gave me temporary respite though, and I trudged along. The pre-closure upset me then, but in hindsight, I am glad it happened. It helped me completely focus on my topic at hand. I was relieved from the demands of the grant in terms of deadlines, reporting, expense submission and so on.

Although I did a quick math and made sure I had my war chest, I ran out of money faster than I imagined. Despite all my best calculations, I had structural breaks. During this period, my father had a knee replacement surgery. Although I had him covered by insurance, it didn't meet the entire cost. My sister chipped in, but nevertheless it was a sizeable amount of money. Actually, every paisa spent seemed like a major expenditure. My ex driver probably now earned a better salary.

I spread the word amongst my contacts who would talk incessantly about these killer consultancy projects that would probably pay us much more, albeit at just a fraction of the work we were currently doing. "There is this serial entrepreneur who is in need of a financial consultant. You just need to put in a couple of hours a week at your convenient time and he is ready to pay you at X rate per hour or X+ rate per hour and so on."

And I would wonder if I was indeed wasting and whiling my time away at my office. This was just one of the grandiose consultancy opportunities that would be tossed about. It ranged from the sublime to the ridiculous. When I decided to take the plunge of quitting and getting back to studies, I got in touch with these dream merchants to take up one of those touted projects. Believe you me, nothing worked out. Nothing! Strangely, coincidentally, all the offers were put on hold just around the time when I needed it the most. "Something will surely come up and we'll let you know," they told me condescendingly. I am still waiting to hear from them.

I reassessed my investment portfolio which was left in the able hands of professional investment consultants. I had no time to review and analyse it. Now I took over, had the time to initiate discussions and debate with them over their suggestions. I finally felt I was getting in complete control of my finances.

Lifestyle changes

The hi's and hellos to friends and acquaintances also reduced. Basically, I decided it was not important to wish all and sundry and focused on keeping in regular touch only with a chosen few. Temptations like WhatsApp and Facebook were kept at bay. I was neither a WhatsApp nor Facebook victim, so it was no big deal. I was also not into posting inane stuff such as 'checked into Flying Elephant,' 'taking my dog to the spa,' 'upholstery shopping at Jamaals,' etc. Who cared?

I basically indulged in a digital detox. In any case, if your friends and relatives are truly your well-wishers, they will understand, and others who don't are definitely not your well-wishers so it doesn't matter.

It's a pity that when one has the money, one doesn't have the time and vice versa. The house that I had bought with so much love and pride had been neglected. A full-time career and taking care of my father took away most of my time. While in the case of my friends, their children were grown up and needed less monitoring; in my case, it was the reverse with my father getting old and entering his second childhood, thus requiring more monitoring. And as I was living with him, it required real-time monitoring, not remote monitoring.

I could now take better care of my health as well, while making sure he didn't miss his doctor's appointments. I had time to engage with my father more gainfully than ever before. I strived to give him a more stable and secure environment. Basically, it involved realigning my priorities. I rediscovered my old hobbies, renewed ties with some friends with whom I had lost touch, had time to assess certain relationships and cut off those who had become the proverbial albatross around the neck.

"You are the average of the 5 people you spend the most time with," said Jim Rohn, the American entrepreneur, author and motivational speaker. *"Hence, choose these people with utmost care."*

For a year and a half, I was busy with classes, quizzes and my hobbies. I didn't have to succumb to a 9 to 5 routine and that seemed like such a relief. I left from home depending on my class timings and my meetings with my guide. I had a flexible schedule and could catch up on my afternoon nap sometimes, which was such a luxury. I started having more home-cooked food. I could have lunch with my father at regular intervals. Of course, like college students, I too hung around with other researchers in the mess and had my share of ice-creams, pastas, chat, etc., and enjoyed every bit of it.

I did not suffer Monday blues anymore. I had time to renew and continue my morning walks. I could watch the sunrise on the beach and sit on a bench and savour it, while some of my friends were rushing back from their morning walks to get ready to go to office, or worse still didn't have the luxury of a morning walk.

My friend, who was a big shot in an MNC and was bulging both in terms of salary and girth, used to leave home at 6.45 am and head to his office on the outskirts of Chennai. I would get a cheap thrill in calling him around that time when I would be on my morning walk at the beach and waxing eloquently, almost poetically, about the ascent of the golden God.

Coursework and quizzes

When I entered the classroom after more than a decade, I entered the classroom with a lot of trepidation. The classroom was filled with youngsters and it gave me the heebie-jeebies.

Armed with lofty ideals and research ideas, I was thrown into the whirlpool. The students and several researchers were half my age and I felt like a senior citizen. I discarded my sarees, lest I got confused with a professor.

When I entered, I almost felt that the class would rise and greet me, thinking I was a Prof, as in the movie *Munnabhai MBBS*. Thankfully no such thing happened and I quickly settled in the first bench. The class went on for an hour and some 30 minutes… or was it 40 minutes? I couldn't tell for sure. Half an hour into the class, my mind started wandering. I had no clue as to what had transpired after that. I just zoned out for the rest of the class. I was mentally and physically exhausted by the end of day one. I learnt that each class would last for an hour and 50 minutes. And I had signed up for 4 courses for that first semester. Would I really survive this onslaught?

Classes were followed by more classes. Then there were assignments, projects, surprise quizzes and end-term exams. Gosh, it tired me. Co-ordinating with these MBA kids for assignments was a nightmare. Having come from a corporate culture where we were ready with our deliverables at least one day prior to the deadline, this eleventh-hour, knee-jerk preparation got me all worked up. There were times when we dashed into an 8 am class after having completed our assignment at 7.58 am.

In one of the classes, for one of the assignments that had a high weightage, we had a simulated game where we had to run our company under different circumstances with different capital structures. I was teamed up with 2 other supposedly not-so-strong candidates. The idea was that I should guide them and help them. The game was completed 4 weeks later. We came last. My ego lay in tatters now. I realised this was just the beginning.

Being constantly in the company of young people made me feel energetic and lively. But sometimes I also missed the company of people my age. One day when I had some free time and I was chit-chatting with these youngsters, one girl walked towards us with her wedding invite in her hand. "Please do come" to all in general and to me in particular she said, "Please do come, AUNTY." Ouch! It hurt!

The campus was also home to simians. I saw these monkeys flitting from one branch to the other. They pounced on unsuspecting people and stole their water bottles, lunchboxes, etc. They sometimes accompanied us to class. They perched themselves on the windowsills and seemed to be listening in rapt attention with an expressionless visage.

Sitting in a classroom with young kiddos, appearing for quizzes, cramming for the mid-term exams and end-term exams is not everyone's cup of tea. Not all can take the heat. My famed memory which was the envy of my friends in the good old days failed me dismally when I needed it the most. Had age really caught up? After a long gap, I was sleeping late and waking early to prepare for an exam.

Having been an A-lister all through, it was a huge blow to my ego when I got a B grade for the first time in my life. It really upset me. I also felt embarrassed. Then, I got used to it! "At least I didn't get a C," I consoled myself. I began to wonder if my previous academic achievements were just a pipe dream. I probably suffered from an imposter syndrome.

I remember a tough stats (statistics for the uninitiated) class where I felt everything going 10 ft over my head. I was distraught. I struggled through the course. I had hesitatingly convinced myself that I was indeed going to earn my first ever C. I forewarned my guide as well. When the results were out, there was a flurry of activity with my classmates informing me that one had to go to the Prof's cabin and find out their respective grades. Fellow students scurried to meet the Prof, yet I was in no hurry. I didn't go and find out.

Someone later told me that the Prof. was wondering why I hadn't come to find out about my grade as I was the only person left to do so. Finally, I mustered some courage and went to her cabin and she told me in a very consoling tone that I had secured a B. I broke into a smile and confused her thoroughly. Later in the elevator, I bumped into my classmate who looked sullen because she had got an A and not S! Tsk Tsk! When she asked me my grade, I triumphantly said, "I got a B! Yippee!"

With more disposable time in the first year, I found myself multi-tasking. I was doing several things simultaneously and marvelled at my own ability to manage. I didn't realise that I was getting stressed in the bargain. Balancing several things and wanting to give my best shot in all was taking its toll. I felt fatigued. I was doing a lot but achieving less. My attention span was shrinking. I was unnecessarily straining my hippocampus. I decided to reduce my mental cacophony. I proceeded to close all the tabs that I had opened in my life that were causing me to slow down.

The research journey

My area of interest had to be mapped with what would be palatable to researchers, what was the current flavour and my guide's interest and expertise. It was not easy to arrive at a consensus. I wanted to conduct breakthrough research. I wanted to work in the field of corporate finance. Something relevant to the kind of experience and exposure I had gained in my corporate stint, definitely something to do with Corporate Governance.

My guide and I tweaked my research topic based on feedback from my doctoral committee and based on the latest trends in my chosen topic. There would have been some overlap in work had the CA project continued. Now I plunged headlong into my topic.

The library at the department and the central library was a reservoir of an excellent collection of books and materials and I devoured them with great enthusiasm. Literature review is a long winding process of surfing through tons and tons of research papers published in top journals by top authors on the chosen topic of your research. It is the due diligence that also signals to the audience that a thorough survey and analysis of work done in the similar field has been exhaustively and comprehensively reviewed. It is one of the key academic requirements.

One obviously doesn't want that the research one is planning on has already been dealt with in depth and that too some aeons ago. One reviews and analyses the research topic, methodology, findings, applicability, relevance, etc. The importance of a thorough review cannot be overemphasised. It helps in your research getting the necessary focus and shape as it gives you new insights and perspectives. The literature that has been quoted in your dissertation needs to be compiled and stated under the 'References' heading that normally appears in the bibliography at the end and has a specific format.

I tried working in the scholar's lab where different researchers in different disciplines and different research areas vied with each other. Some had a glazed look, while some would stare blankly at you. Others would wax eloquently about how their paper got selected in the first round. It was enough to deflate someone who had been rejected umpteen times. People would debate and deliberate incessantly and it affected both my morale and concentration.

I escaped to the safe environ of the MBA lab. Although the kids were too boisterous, it helped that they had frequent classes and I would devour those precious moments of silence that made me think clearly. It also helped that no one knew me and so they left me alone. There was no disturbance and that is what I precisely needed. I made friends with Moduru Bala Bheem Sagar (only 1 person) who was 1 year into his research and also worked in the MBA lab.

Research is a lonely profession and you need to slog till you see some light and make some sense out of it. The guides and mentors can give top level guidance but since there's no handholding, one is pretty much on one's own. One needs to keep track of what one's doing else it's easy to get lost or waste time in repeated tests. Unless one's guide is up for promotion and needs to ensure she has graduated few of her scholars, there is no one in a tearing hurry that you finish fast. It's all up to the individual to push herself. Unlike in a 9 to 5 job where someone is breathing down your neck and you have these darned deadlines for each and every activity, no one is bothered and there are no milestones to achieve or anyone to question you.

One needs to have extreme self-motivation. There are people who have been on this journey for some 5 years and more, counting. Mon Dieu! God bless them. Leonard Cassuto, a professor of English at Fordham University, has highlighted the disturbing trend of only 50 percent of doctoral students actually completing their course.

Lofty ideas are fine but one needs a guide to nudge you in the right direction else you might tie yourself up in knots. The question I most dreaded by my colleagues was, "So how is it going?" This was a rhetorical question, which deserved a rhetorical answer. "Don't even ask!" I would answer and slip away.

Rule #1: *Never ask a researcher how their research is progressing*

I spent more time at home flipping through research papers and figuring out what and how I was exactly going to go about my research. I would sometimes hide in the cafeteria, cry on my friend's shoulder in her hostel room or go for random solitary walks. Sometimes, when we encountered obstacles, we cried on each other's shoulders. It helped that she was doing her research in OB & HR. Researchers make for strange bedfellows. A kind of implied silent solidarity creeps in amongst the researchers.

It's important to accept that research is a never-ending activity. There will be innumerable methodologies to tackle the problem on hand. If we choose Method A, sometimes co-researchers and other professors will wonder why we didn't use Method B or C and vice versa. As long as we are clear in our heads as to why we have used Method A and are able to reasonably justify it, fear not.

I had to equip myself with quantitative data analysis, statistics and econometrics. I attended few workshops and classes, poured over books and interacted with my guide and co-researchers. There was a general talk in the lab that this person was a pro at econometrics. I diligently and shamelessly pestered her for her time. After the interaction I realised that though she knew quite a bit, it wasn't enough. If my knowledge level was 10%, hers was probably 50%, optimistically stating. So, I still had hope.

I would meet my guide frequently to discuss my progress. I would have these tables in Excel with my findings and their interpretations. "Well, not bad. Continue." Or else it would be, "This cannot work. Redo. These variables are just not sufficient."

And I would walk out like an injured tiger licking my wounds. These high-level comments were something I would eventually get used to. It's up to the researcher to figure out the inner meaning and arrive at some relevant conclusions. A lot of it didn't make sense to me initially. I struggled and then struggled even more, and then I found a way out.

I read and re-read but couldn't gain meaningful insights sometimes and couldn't connect the dots. I lived in an ivory tower. No one knew what I was going through. I wasn't quite sure that I knew myself. I hit roadblocks with alarming alacrity. The data had to be cleaned and further cleaned. Outliers abounded. Data unavailability, incomplete data, varying data… you name it and I had faced it. I shed frustrated tears.

I sometimes wondered what the hell I was doing. Was my research really going to bring about some fundamental change in the corporate world or in the world in general? Why then was I slogging, with practically nil income, when I could have continued in my cushy job where my salary would get credited at the end of the month with regularity?

I barely slept peacefully at night. I frequently snapped at my father. I was turning into a werewolf. I avoided Facebook initially and eventually left it. Some friends posted fancy pictures posing in front of the Eiffel Tower, skydiving at Prague, visiting the Vatican and so on. And here I was thinking twice about taking an Ola cab or an auto while travelling within Chennai!

When I recited my prayers, which I now did rather regularly and with renewed devotion, I found myself thinking more about my guide than the pantheon of gods. All those romantic notions of sipping cappuccino and doling out research *gyan* couldn't be farther from the truth.

One of my fellow scholars pronounced that she was interested in researching on how and why private banks are more profitable than public sector banks. Well this could be termed as an interesting topic; however, it has to be described at a granular level. It is too wide a topic and one could get lost. Some of the research topics require translation. It's not clear what the research is all about and sometimes it's not clear what is researchable on a particular topic! Some of them are unwittingly funny on the other hand and the less said about them the better.

The doctor's doctor

I developed mysterious ailments along the way. I had a fancy sounding condition which doctors termed tennis elbow. I hadn't even heard of this thing before. The doc educated me about this and also mentioned in passing that Sachin Tendulkar had also been afflicted by this condition. Now, we were talking! I was almost proud of my condition now. Finally I had something in common with Sachin Tendulkar.

This tennis elbow thingie normally inflicted sportspeople. Why then did I get it? The doctors were equally clueless. Treatment started and continued. 2 weeks and 7000 bucks later, I didn't find much difference. I decided to ignore the pain.

Next, I developed an eye-related issue that even surgery couldn't fix. After trying many treatments, I returned to homeopathy and was cured. Clearly, the placebo effect, concluded some people.

I was also down with viral fever quite a few times during this period. I was a witness to such mysterious ailments that afflicted my friends and colleagues as well. One of the researchers took a 2-month sabbatical as her BP went north and another took an annual leave citing some other ailment. Was it stress created by the system, guide's expectations or self-inflicted stress? Who knows!

Trudging along

As I was neck-deep in my research, I had isolated myself. Some friends who were irked with me stopped calling me while some understood when I explained to them that I now inhabited a different world. People do understand if you explain to them. Yes, there is always a risk that you will be ostracised but that's a risk you will need to take. I didn't have the time or the energy to explain the situation to them.

I found more time to engage with my father. I experimented with different dishes and I watched his favourite shows with him. We argued, we fought, we sulked like a normal family. But we coped.

I attended Bhagavad Geeta classes which were held at IIT and this really helped to calm the storm which sometimes raged inside me. From a reactive person who would snap at the slightest provocation, I learnt to ignore these and focus on my goal a la Arjuna. I now frequently indulged in pollyannaish gyan. Que sera sera.

Reigniting dormant hobbies

Learning Hindustani music had been a secret desire of mine as I had dabbled with it briefly during my school days. I located a teacher who was both a great singer and a wonderful teacher. Classes were on a one-to-one basis and charges, although justified for the quality teaching, were definitely on the higher side. I didn't mind it as I was getting good lessons from an extremely competent teacher.

I sojourned in the realm of *Raag Bageshree*. Then followed the beautiful *Raag Nat Bhairav*, a perfect fusion of *Raag Nat* and *Raag Bhairav*. The ethos of the raag was distinctly pathos but coated with touches of exhilaration. Wasn't it Shakespeare who said, *"If music be the food of love, play on?"*

It really is nourishment for the soul. I listened in a trance as my teacher sang so beautifully. Once, during my class, I was singing the *sargams* and *bandish* with full involvement and gusto, when my guru told me that I had drifted from *Raag Nat Bhairav* to *Raag Ahir Bhairav* without even realising it. Apparently, I hit a wrong note and this one wrong note made all the difference.

The class timings were sacrosanct. But sometimes, assignments, quizzes and studies crept in, making it difficult to keep up the schedule. Further, in order to advance in my lessons, I needed to practice religiously on a regular basis for which I couldn't find the time or the mind space. With the result, I was not progressing and also getting chided by my teacher. I was being compared to some kids who were grasping better and advancing faster. I realised I was only getting stressed and decided to discontinue temporarily.

In the meantime, I renewed my dance classes. I decided to learn Kathak since I had learnt Bharatanatyam during my school days. Hindustani music and Kathak is a lethal combination. I felt like Meena Kumari in *Pakeezah* when I wore the *ghungroos*. I loved the graceful hand movements, the rhythmic foot movements and the *adahs* which are so typical of a Kathak dance.

All went well till the twirls started. Initially it was at a manageable pace and I enjoyed it. Before long, the speed increased and I found my head spinning long after I stopped twirling. Sometimes I started the twirls at a particular spot in the room and when I finished and looked around, I realised I was in another part of the room. How I crossed over to the other side is a mystery I am yet to solve. But it was so much fun. I continued the classes for well over a year till the venue of the classes got shifted to a far-off place.

But what I realised was that if one badly needs to do something, one should just go ahead and do it.

Where's the money honey?

Time flies and so does money. My savings and safety net evaporated even before I could say Jack Robinson. Although I had mentally prepared myself for some short-term volatility, reality hit hard. My net worth was eroding rapidly. I was probably in the grip of a bear run.

In any case, what great savings can a middle-class working professional hope to have? Wealth creation for a working professional didn't quite take off until the late 90s and that too if you were employed with an IT company, MNC or a financial services company. With the pathetic tax structure, fewer avenues for tax savings and the ridiculously low tax breaks available, what can one possibly save? The conveyance deduction was still fixed at a princely sum of Rs 800 per month and we have errant unfettered auto drivers charging more than that on a single trip although the fare should be worth half or one-fourth of the amount.

I had calculated the bare amount of money I would require when I decided to take a break. On hindsight, I realised that after one has arrived at the amount of money required to meet fixed expenses, one should straightaway multiply it by 2. This is likely to be the realistic estimate of the money that will be required to keep your head above the water. My father would oft say, "Our generation had health but no wealth and your generation has amassed wealth but sacrificed health."

I needed some cash flow but had little time to spare. It entailed taking up an assignment much below my station as it wouldn't involve too much of my time but help me to keep the fire burning. I decided I would provide advice to a start-up on how to clean up their accounts. It felt a tad demeaning at times but then I didn't have too many choices. I wanted to charge for every wee bit of advice I was doling out. Days of pro bono advice were over.

One of my ex-colleagues came up with a bright idea. A newly listed company was in need of a Chief financial officer (CFO), on paper, but didn't want one in reality as they felt it was not required at the stage and in any case they couldn't afford one. So they wanted to appoint a CA as a CFO but pay him only a token amount as he was not required on a daily basis, actually not required at all, except to sign some odd statements and of course the mother of all statements – the audited financial statements. I was asked if I would be interested in taking this up. I baulked. I felt insulted. Did they really think I would stoop to this level?

Desperate acts require desperate measures. In order to save money, I decided to chuck my maid. She was anyway doing a shoddy job and giving me ulcers by not keeping to time, taking off at her will, discussing her never-ending problems and so on. I decided that since the work was minimal, I need not pay her and also put up with her tardiness. So, out she went.

I was really proud of myself. My penny pinching had crawled up a notch higher. However, a couple of months down the line, I realised it was a huge mistake. Sweeping and mopping was not my forte and it was aggravating my dust allergy. Such jobs are best outsourced which releases the time that can be spent on your core areas. I hired another maid and although the shoddiness continued, I decided to turn a blind eye and focused on the critical work on hand. I also ensured that the maid walked in only after I left for the university. This way I could avoid aggravating my ulcers.

I also resorted to taking public transport more often in a bid to avoid getting fleeced by the auto drivers. I travelled by bus, chased buses and jostled with fellow passengers. I was embarrassed on being spotted by a friend who drove in her swanky car as poor me waited at the bus-stop. Initially I felt very sorry for myself but every penny saved was a penny earned.

In some odd, inexplicable way, I sometimes enjoyed these bus journeys. It gave me time to look around, ruminate and soak in. During one such journey, I noticed that right in the centre of a busy area some builder had started construction of sprawling mammoth apartments. *A niche apartment for the riche*, screamed the hoardings. The construction commenced and grew at a rapid pace. I saw with concern as the landscape was dominated by this apartment. When I was 2 months shy of completing 18 months, the construction was completed with the beautiful view blocked. The skyline had receded further and now the high-rise apartment stood like a stubborn Godzilla.

I sometimes hitched a ride with my fellow researchers. Riding on the potholed roads, I sometimes felt like I was on a horse. "Don't crib," warned my colleague. "Remember, you ain't paying taxes this year." But what about the huge taxes I had paid in the past? During better times, I took Ola Share sometimes. When an ever-intrusive fellow Indian passenger asked me, "What are you doing?" I would state, "I am pursuing my PhD." Amongst the range of responses I received, one really stood out for its sheer innovation. One passenger actually asked "Why?" Now how does one answer such a profound question!

My trips to the parlours also reduced and I realised it was such a substantial saving. Earlier I would get sweet talked into availing extra services which I didn't even need. Now I almost carried a placard which shouted "**I only want a haircut and nothing else**. So don't sell me your miscellaneous fancy sounding services." Out went that quarterly trip to the fancy saloon for an insanely expensive haircut. In any case, I was back to the same curly and uneven mop after one wash.

What then was the point if I didn't have the time and patience to maintain it the way it was styled? Those herbal, golden pedicures were also given a royal miss. I successfully thwarted all attempts by the parlour girls. They anyway didn't seem too pleased to see me as I never tipped them. The ever-increasing service cost, plus the service tax, this tax, that tax and then we are expected to top it up with a tip as well? This was one recession-proof industry. I discovered a parlour at the campus itself which charged just a fraction of what the other parlours would charge, and I switched parlours immediately.

I could no longer indulge in this extravaganza. I didn't know if I was frugal or plain stingy. But I definitely wasn't dirt-bagging it. I would often bump into my ex-office colleagues or old colleagues dressed to kill with shiny noses, blushed cheeks and gelled hair. And I would be a trifle conscious of my bordering on shabby and dowdy attire.

I had the option of renting my home and shifting to a room in the institute. It would have been a big saving as my house would have fetched a decent sum as rent given its prime location. But again, I didn't want to dislodge my father.

I realised how much food I was wasting, how many unwanted and unused items I was hoarding. It made me extremely guilty. I continued paying my EMIs (equated monthly instalments) as I was lucky to have got a loan at a relatively cheaper interest rate. Dining out trickled down to once in 6 months or became an annual affair, that too at a reasonably priced hotel. A couple of close friends picked up the tab whenever we met during this phase. It hurt my ego terribly and I was worried about being branded a freeloader.

I analysed my spending patterns, which revealed some interesting insights. You realise the whopping amount of money you spend on these transitory things. I wanted my credit card to disappear. It didn't. So I did the next best thing. I vandalised it with great glee and chucked it in the trashcan.

Around that time, a global ice cream vendor set shop in Chennai. Being an avid ice cream lover (who isn't?), I promptly crash-landed there. One look at the menu card and I turned ashen. The cheapest ice cream cost 800 bucks. Now who eats ice cream for 800 bucks? Turns out, a lot of people. 800 bucks for molten puddle? Hmm...

Another evening, I accompanied a friend to a dance programme that was in aid of some charity. She told me that donating was optional. I decided to refrain from donating. I could do with some donation myself. People all around me were writing cheques for 1000 bucks or more. I felt very cheap but I stood my ground. Charity is sometimes so expensive...

Rule # 2: *Never ask a researcher how they are managing their finances*

That year, December 1st was a black day, literally, in Chennai with the incessant rain and winds wailing like a banshee. Chennai was up with everybody contributing and helping out in every which way they could. I too did my bit by distributing food and some old clothes. My maid kept throwing hints as to how the other employers had given her 5k, 3k and so on. I gave a benign smile in return. That was all I gave her.

Compri

I managed to complete the required 16 credits from my courses, which opened the doors to the next phase. I was now qualified to dive deep into my research. Soon after came the time for the dreaded 'Comprehensive Viva voce' exam or 'Compri' in research lingo. Horror stories were afloat on how tough it would be and so on. I was a bundle of nerves as I studied and revised.

Mock compri sessions ensued where my colleagues had a field day throwing probable questions at me and watching me wince. I felt I was about to erupt like Eyjafjallajökull (How does one even pronounce this?).

My sister offered to take care of my father while I battled with my books and my fear. I was all alone at home. To ensure uninterrupted time and avoid pesky, unwanted visitors – courier boys, wannabe salespeople, vendors – I asked my friend to lock me in my own house. When she gave me an incredulous look, I simply told her, "We live in India. We don't have a right to privacy. Please lock me up and open the door only when I ask you to."

Having taken care of the administration issues, I now prepared hard. I had rehearsals and timed myself repeatedly until I could almost recite the presentation backwards. We had a prescribed syllabus based on the courses we took and I prepared extensively from various reference books. Two days before the compri, I was told that there was no such thing as a syllabus and the panel could test me from any course, irrespective of whether I had taken the course or not. Wow!

When the D day finally arrived, I was on the verge of a nervous breakdown. I had told my family members and friends not to wish me as it would make me more nervous. I entered the frosty room (some called it the gas chamber) and made sure everything was in order. As the clock ticked and my heartbeat increased, members from my doctoral committee walked in. There were about 7 of them in toto.

I had secretly hoped, rather cheaply, that 1 or 2 would be absent. But that was not to be. 7 pairs of stern eyes turned towards me. I took a deep breath, made my presentation and waited for the onslaught. Questions followed. Then more questions followed. Some I answered convincingly; some I couldn't. I was then politely asked to wait outside.

As I waited outside, I encountered some of my curious fellow researchers who were eager to know what transpired. After what seemed like an eternity, I was summoned inside. 7 sullen faces greeted me and I thought it was a nay. The whole process was a blur and all that I could recall was being told that I had cleared. That's all that mattered at the end of the day, although I felt I could have done much better. Also, the way the news was conveyed to me confused me.

I was told about a series of things that were not in order and finally in a sotto voce I was told that I had cleared the viva voce. Talk about a left-handed compliment. I realised that whether in a corporate or in academics, people are parsimonious with compliments. Nevertheless, it was one milestone crossed.

This was the signal for me to plunge headlong into research and produce good work. If I thought I had cleared the tough part of my programme, I was in for a surprise, a really big one.

The data collection and data cleaning were excruciating. I had to painstakingly collect and collate data. Although Prowess is acknowledged as the standard package, I ran into roadblocks several times as the data was not available or incomplete. I then had to revert to company websites to scan through their annual reports. In doing so, I sometimes found that the data collected for a period from Prowess was different from what appeared in the annual report. The sheer amount of data to be collected, collated and cleaned overwhelmed me. Different sources had to be used to validate the accuracy of the data collected.

I ran some basic models to study the results, but they didn't reveal any insights. I discovered a non-linear relationship between the efforts I put in and the results I obtained. I had to again go to the data, clean it up, look for multicollinearity, heteroskedasticity (you read it right), autocorrelation and so on.

The manual labour involved infuriated me and I wondered what I was doing as the exercise continued for months on end. I was in an unfamiliar world and felt completed alienated. Each was battling with his own issues and so help was hardly forthcoming.

Statistics was a subject that I had avoided and now it was here to plague me. Econometrics was another giant that I had to encounter. When I threw up my hands in sheer frustration, my guide would constantly remind me, "And you thought research was so simple? You know it took me 2 years to really understand what I was doing and what I wanted to do."

She made me feel so average. How mean! It doesn't take you long to realise that you are damn alone in this and you had darn well accept it. A guide's job is to guide and not toil with you in the fields. 24/7 I was working on my research, thinking about my research or wondering what the hell I was doing.

I went into a shell and very often had a glazed and disoriented look that my family found very disconcerting. I was afflicted with 'PhD-iositis,' or some condition like that, which affects most researchers. I started doing research even in my dreams. There was just no respite. Even if I forcibly distracted myself, I almost immediately began to have withdrawal symptoms. Several months of non-stop struggle later, I managed small victories, some modicum of success.

Yet, you solve one problem only to run into another. The initial work also resulted in my guide realigning my work based on feedback from my committee and our study on the contemporary work done world over. Though we had planned to do quite a bit, our committee warned us about the enormity of the task we were aiming at and asked us to truncate it.

Although initially we held our heads high and refused to budge, the initial results and requirement of valid data made us rethink and we truncated and tweaked our work a bit. I had panic attacks. Did my work really qualify as good research, or as research itself? Surely, research meant something more meaningful than this? Wasn't it my aim to do groundbreaking research?

Nevertheless, I had jumped in and now I had to swim or sink. I also had palpitations. What if I decided to give up mid-way out of sheer anxiety or worse still, non-performance? I adopted one banyan tree. Many frustrated days were spent under the warm confines of this banyan tree, waiting for some holy soul up there to do *'maarg darshan.'* My veritable bodhi tree.

The third year was uneventful. I was running like a headless chicken. I felt as if I was on a treadmill and walking at an increasing pace but not reaching anywhere. By the end of the third year, the pressure had mounted exponentially. Some nosy relatives wanted to know when I would finish though I was just a little over 2 years into my PhD. My father got pressurised by the constant nagging and questioning by these relatives. He would constantly get worked up and would keep urging me to focus and complete it at the earliest.

Rule # 3: *Never ask a researcher when they are likely to complete their PhD*

Finally, I had to summon my co-researcher who came home and patiently explained to my father about how the research world had changed, and although the resources were plenty, the requirements and stress were also plenty. My father was temporarily appeased, but only temporarily.

Four months down the line, due to the cascading effect, the concerned questioning commenced. With the constant reminders about my status, I was in a tearing hurry to finish and announce to the world that I was done. But you know what? No one gives a damn. People just need some juicy story to talk about.

One such example was when I met a realtor who asked me what I was doing. When I rather proudly told her that I was pursuing my research, she asked me with a deadpan expression if it was useful? Now, how useful is useful?

Despite these setbacks, just when I thought I had to fine-tune my work a wee bit, my guide declared, "Maybe we should try some additional methodology, additional data…" Immediately, I had visions of an additional 6 months and my heart did a weak somersault…

Publish or Perish

Intense pressure to publish hangs like a Damocles sword over your head. There is mounting pressure to publish in these 1500 (and counting) journals which are sadly only read by and accessible to a select few.

And I hadn't even started writing a paper… The thumb rule was that it would take a year to do some meaningful work and write a paper. My guide had identified a journal which had called for papers pertaining to my area of research. The deadline came and went and we were nowhere near some decent output. Few such journals deadlines were missed. Finally we made some headway and sent an abstract to another conference as no relevant journal was forthcoming.

While several of my colleagues' abstracts got selected, mine was rejected. My first rejection. I was depressed. The fact that my colleagues had their paper accepted made the depression worse. I sent my first paper in March 2015 which was 3 ¼ years since I began my research. This was really lousy by any standard. Most of my colleagues had sent 2 papers by then. People say that if you want anything badly, the whole universe conspires for you to get it. Why was this not working in my case?

Rule # 4: Never ask a researcher if they have got their first research paper published

Writing the paper was a process in itself. I had prided myself on my writing skills which were about to be shattered to smithereens. "Your writing is too corporate, too flowery." How my writing could be both was unfathomable, but nevertheless, I was torn asunder. I didn't have an EGO anymore. Not even a semblance.

It's not enough if one just completes writing a paper. The guide will go through it and clear it; she may even modify it to such an extent that it won't even remotely resemble your original paper. Then it has to go through a plagiarism check. Then it is sent to an editor who will edit it and send it back after a couple of weeks. Then it is burnished further and finally it is ready to be sent. By then, you couldn't care less if it is accepted or not.

There is a cut-throat academic publishing world out there and one needs to be really up on the game of what is the hot and contemporary topic and whether there are any special issues of journal requiring your kind of papers. Getting passionate and emotional about one's topic is not enough.

I almost immediately started work on my 2nd paper and sent it in Nov'15 to a conference's special issue. It got accepted. Hallelujah! I heaved a sigh of relief after what seemed like an eternity. Finally some stray light at the end of the tunnel. Getting the first paper accepted by a peer-reviewed journal can be a defining moment for a researcher.

No news in sight from the editor of the journal for the paper sent in Mar'15. Now I couldn't care less as a major requirement was ticked off the checklist. I suddenly was on 4th gear. My third paper, 2 seminars and a synopsis followed in quick succession. Now I was ready for my synopsis, which is the penultimate stage of your PhD. I was now just one viral fever away from clearing my synopsis.

By the time one reaches the synopsis stage one it is expected to have the draft thesis ready. You look with pride at your thesis, the summation of years of toil, self-doubt, panic, frustration, exhilaration and what not. During the synopsis, you present your entire work to a committee which comprises of your DC members and which is chaired by the Dean of Academic Research. This is to re-assess whether the work you have done qualifies as decent work and is good enough to be recommended to be sent to external examiners for review.

Post synopsis, when I was told that I could submit my thesis, I almost kissed the ground. After several months, I slept peacefully that night. Less than a month later, I scurried to the office with the bound copies of the thesis. I was scared to glance through it one last time lest I found some error.

Conferences

One of my papers got selected for a conference at Vietnam and then at Luneburg. The conference at Vietnam was a much-needed change for me. I hobnobbed with fellow researchers and professors from different management schools all over the world. The gala dinner was eventful. The entire animal kingdom was on the menu. Even for a hardcore non-vegetarian, the spread would have been a trifle exotic. I safely stuck to a fruit diet.

I had decided to extend my stay couple of days post the conference to explore the city.

I had a whale of a time and it was a novel experience to enjoy a trip without bothering about pesky calls from an irritating boss or having to log on to the laptop or peer into the phone to check on emails every now and then and expected to reply pronto. On the city tour, I bumped into this 30 something guy from the US. He was an avid player in the stock market and had made pot loads of money by trading in some penny stocks. In fact, he made so much money that he quit his job and decided to travel the world. He didn't have any plan and said he was exploring Vietnam for the past week or so.

When asked where he was headed next, he shrugged his shoulders and said, "Who knows? Depends on my mood!" Sigh! What a life!

The second conference saw me in Luneburg, Germany a quaint little town tucked away from the crowded city. I enjoyed the peace and quiet and made some new friends. I wondered with barely concealed envy as to how the locals looked like they had just stepped out of a sauna even after a hard day's work, while I was a dishevelled wreck by then. As is wont in these conferences, we seek out fellow researchers from other countries who are researching similar topics. Some alliances and partnerships are forged with the intention to jointly do research and publish papers in top-notch journals.

Defence viva

The Defence is the final rite of passage. One hour before s/he is a researcher and one hour later s/he is a doctorate. How life changes in that short span of time! I looked with contempt at all those who were 'conferred' a doctorate. Is it so easily available? At the Defence, the scholar starts with a glowing tribute to his guide. He attributes every modicum of his success to his guide and lays it squarely at his feet.

The examiners would ask some pertinent questions on the thesis which would be needed to be defended convincingly and humbly. Such an oxymoron. A tall task indeed. The stage is all yours. And you have to give your best performance. The room is expected to be packed with research scholars who are in various stages of their research. There will be faculty from your subject's department and even other departments. After all, the information regarding the defence is out in the open.

When I completed the defence, I was asked to wait outside. I waited with bated breath. Normally, only in the rarest of rarest cases does something go awry at this stage. When I was summoned inside and told that I had cleared the defence viva and was addressed as Dr Geeta, I burst into tears, especially when my guide hugged me. I felt an ownership and a sense of pride... tears of relief... tears of joy. After the agony comes the ecstasy which more than compensates for the prolonged periods of despair and self-doubt. I wished I could wear the degree as an epaulette.

Things proceed very fast thereafter. You surrender your ID card (very reluctantly), your mail id is disabled, your access to the library is also blocked. Overnight the university becomes your alma mater. You are now an alumni. The suddenness of it is very painful. You want to hold on and not cut the umbilical cord. I felt choked. But life has to go on as they say.

Convocation

And then the day dawned, 22nd of July, the day of the convocation... a day that would be etched in my memory forever. It was almost surreal. I proudly carried my gown with me like it was a trophy and reached the venue with my father, my inspiration for doing my PhD, and sister in tow. My wonderful friend who had come down from Bangalore also accompanied me. The place was throbbing with beaming parents and students who were graduating. The excitement was palpable. It was an important milestone in everybody's life. I had worn a saree... Finally I didn't mind being seen in one.

To my surprise, I realised that of all the students from my department who were getting their degree that day, I had apparently taken the 'least' time to complete. Really? The man with the 4 names (Moduru Bala Bheem Sagar) was also present with me to collect his degree.

After the mandatory ceremonies, the names of the graduating students from different disciplines were called in a particular order. And then, before I realised, my name was called out. The names were called out in such quick succession that by the time I reached centre stage I was collecting Arvind's degree. I anyway walked ecstatically and collected my degree from our director. Shutterbugs clicked for a few seconds. My Kodak moment. I only hoped that my father and sister caught a good glimpse of this. Getting the coveted Dr appended to one's name is awesome to say the least.

Now that I was armed with my degree, I could explore the academic world. My defence examiner told me about the vast options that were available to me. He asked me to send him my updated resume which he said he would forward to the new IIMs and also forward it to his colleagues in other prestigious B-Schools that were on the lookout for people with my credentials. In fact, he did keep his word and I did get a call. But I wasn't so sure if I wanted to take up teaching on a full-time basis. Did I join the academic world or did I do something else? Chapter 7 will explore my decision-making process in detail.

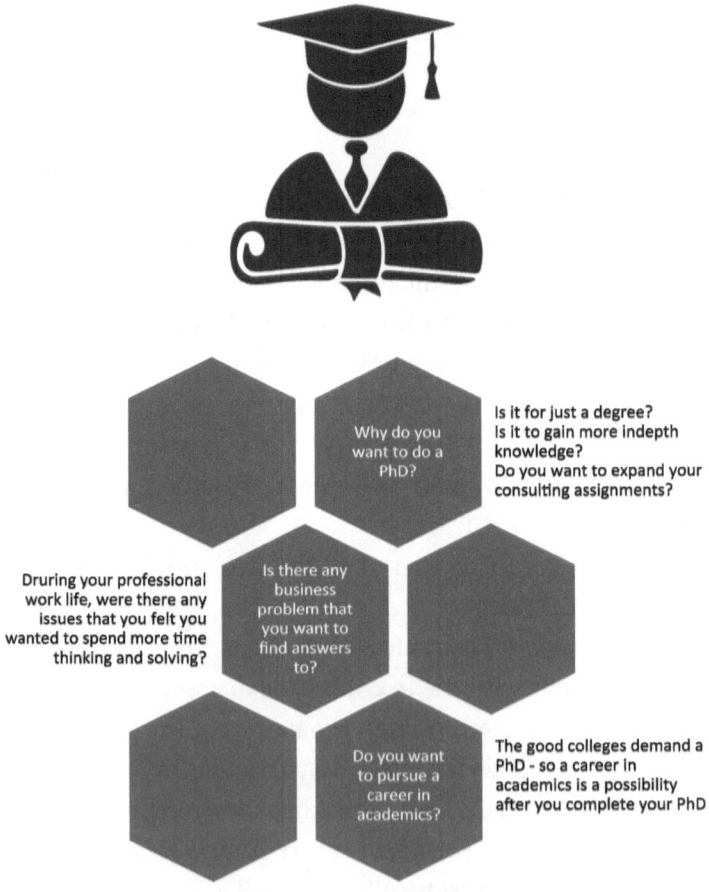

Figure 12: Doing PhD – The critical questions to answer

Chapter 5

Is Academics More Suited for Women?

– *by Rajee*

It is indeed a very subjective question, and honestly, there is no clear answer to it. Academics is more suitable for me as a person, but I cannot answer for every woman and I definitely do not want to generalise it. I have known several successful corporate career women, so I guess it is different strokes for different people. I can however discuss certain research findings which throw some light on this.

In a survey conducted amongst Harvard MBAs, it was found that men and women aimed for and continued to value fulfilling professional and personal lives. However, their ability to realise them according to gender has played out very differently over time. Men are more likely to be in senior management positions than women in corporates and we have seen data evidence of this earlier in the book.

I am quoting 2 examples from the study. A woman in her forties, who left Harvard Business School about 20 years earlier, stated, "For me, at age 25, success in life was defined by *career success*. But now I think of success very differently – raising happy, productive children, contributing to the world around me, and pursuing work that is meaningful to me."

These sentiments were echoed by a man in his fifties, for whom success during his early days was "becoming a highly paid CEO of a medium-to-large business." And today? "Striking a balance between work and family and giving back to society."

Nearly 100% respondents, regardless of gender, said that *quality of personal and family relationships* was 'very' or 'extremely' important. This is an important point – more people seem to value 'relationships' as a very important aspect of success as they grow older.

It was also found that the responsibilities towards child rearing have been a dominant reason for the relatively small percentage of women in corporate boardrooms. The study also reveals that when highly educated professional women leave their jobs after becoming mothers, a very small fraction of them do so because they prefer to devote themselves solely to motherhood; the majority of them leave as a last resort as they find themselves with low career advancement prospects. Also, a large proportion of men expect their partners to take major responsibility for childcare. And more than two-thirds of women actually did so.

This leaves some women with some degree of disappointment and dissatisfaction – that they could not fulfil their dream of a career in spite of initially being ambitious and working hard towards it for several years.

In this context, the choice of academia for women becomes more important. The key advantages of an academic career are:

- the flexible format in which you can chase your intellectual pursuits
- the student bonding experience
- most importantly, the work-life balance as compared to a corporate job

Beyond all this, do I miss the corporate career that I once had? I will discuss this in detail in Chapter 6.

Chapter 6

Corporate vs Academia

Why Rajee loves academics?

I have spent close to 15 years in the industry and have also spent the last 6 years in academia. So I believe that I have the credibility to comment on the much talked about debate on industry vs academia.

Over the last few years, I have read a number of posts talking about the shift of faculty from academia back to the industry. Former professors have blamed low salaries, the difficulty of doing large-scale research, etc., as the reasons for leaving academia. There is some truth to this, but I still feel that it is very one-sided view of academic life, although there is always some truth to the complaints you may read about.

Here are some of my viewpoints on the trade-offs between academia and industry, based on my experience in both realms. First, let's have a look at some of the things that academia has to offer:

One of the most attractive aspects of a job in academia is the freedom that the position offers. As a faculty, you can set out your agenda and have a fair control on how you would be spending the day. This is a huge advantage as it helps to allocate time amongst the tasks from which one would derive the most value. But this also implies that you need to become an expert at time management.

Consulting is another aspect of a faculty's job that allows you to learn about many industries – which may not be possible in corporate. As a consultant, you get into a fair amount of strategic thinking with your clients on their domains and this in turn helps you become a better teacher in the classroom, as you have ample examples as illustrations from real life.

One of the other big differences between industry and academia is the opportunity to work with students. Working with students is probably one of the most rewarding experiences of being a professor that is hard to replicate in other jobs. As a classroom instructor, you have the opportunity to interact with a large number of incredibly bright people who are continually asking questions that shed new light on problems that you've been teaching for years. Working with students and helping them develop their research taste, presentation skills and life skills are simply some of the most meaningful aspects of the job.

Recently, with the opportunity to teach online classes, the opportunity to reach a large number of students has presented itself, which is even more amazing – we now have the opportunity to teach (and influence) an entirely new demographic on a mass scale.

Professors also get to do some real research which is backed by all the resources required that might not be possible without the sponsorship of universities. Activities that transfer research results to the broader society are a part of a professor's mission. To know that your research work has the incredible power of shaping opinions is extraordinary. And a lot of this research work that is original contributes to creating 'new knowledge'.

As an adviser to PhD. students, a professor can shape the professional (and research) development of many students over multiple years. Perhaps even more rewarding is that a professor can regularly learn from students. I have learnt many things about a variety of different areas directly from my students; learning from one's students turns out to be a really exciting and efficient way to learn.

A faculty also has the opportunity to publish books, conduct workshops and seminars, participate in panel discussions and so forth. Basically one can create a lot of intellectual capital. And get to do many versatile things- writing, teaching, researching – all at one go, in your specific area of interest with a fair amount of expertise development. The 'new knowledge' that a faculty creates is both enriching as well as deeply satisfying as it is like leaving a 'knowledge legacy' for generations to come.

Last but not the least advantage that academia enjoys over corporate is the societal respect that the teaching profession commands. The visibility that this profession gives whether it is among the Government bodies, or policy makers or private Institutions or even Internatioanl organisations – is immense. You are regarded highly as an individual and this helps you perform even better.

However, one needs to accept that academics is not a good pay master (compared to corporate in India). It is not an easy journey, especially if monetary requirements and commitments are high. Publication pressure may loom large and that can only be offset by one's passion to wanting to make a meaningful contribution.

Geeta's take on corporate vs Academic career

Earning good money and becoming an academician are almost mutually exclusive (except in a few institutions where one can have a revenue stream of consulting/management development programmes) An assistant professor at the entry level of a top institute could earn anything between Rs 8 lakhs and Rs 10 lakhs a year. That is the average salary of students graduating from most B-Schools in India! I have often wondered how some professors with limited salaries feel when the students they teach get placed in corporates at 6 figure and 7 figure salaries, way higher than theirs.

The selection, especially into the hallowed B-Schools and management schools, is a rigorous process that includes a painfully detailed application, seminar, discussion and interview. The entire process could take close to 6 months. Even if selected, it is most often followed by a 2-year probation period as well. During this period, one needs to obtain a publication in a top-ranked international journal, especially in the top B-Schools, which sometimes acts as a condition precedent to tenure.

During Feb' 2017, the Parliamentary Standing Committee on Human Resource Development (HRD) asked the Department of Higher Education to expedite the process of filling up the vacancies that ranged from well-established central universities to those set up recently, state or private varsities, IITs or IIMs.

The shortage of faculty has been a big handicap in ensuring quality education. The situation continues to be grim with no improvement seen in the near future. The committee pointed out that the existence of vacancies could be attributed to 2 factors: young students not attracted towards the teaching profession or the recruitment process being too prolonged and involving too many procedural formalities. It is also a well-known fact that children of academicians are also not embracing this profession in large numbers.

A country's progress has many a time been directly linked to its research – scientific, economic and even humanitarian. People pursuing their doctorates not only study past trends, but delve deeper into contemporary trends and problems and come up with relevant solutions while creating new knowledge. [Source: The Times of India Delhi; Date: Nov 15, 2010]

A popular misconception is that a PhD is always required to get into academics. The moment one finishes one's PhD, advice pours in galore. Apart from your guide who tries to reveal to you your future path, the well-read academicians and other professors also suggest different academic institutions. Of course, this holds good for those who have continued with their PhD immediately after their masters.

Corporate careers post a PhD are invariably frowned upon by academicians. Most of them are career academicians and have not dabbled in the corporate world. As a freshly minted PhD, the doors to an academic career are wide open, especially if you have earned your spurs from a reputed institution.

Dr Jane Sherwood, Director of Graduate Admissions and Funding, Oxford University, UK, stated: "Apart from academics, doctoral graduates can pursue successful careers in a variety of areas including journalism, broadcasting, education, public administration, law, medicine, finance, consultancy, IT, science, engineering and technology, as well as in the charity and NGO sectors."

My father did his PhD and followed it up with a postdoc overseas. Had he continued there, he would have definitely signed up for an academic career. He returned to India like a dutiful son and veered towards the more pragmatic choice of a corporate career although his heart lay in academics.

In academics, there is comparatively more freedom and flexibility. You are not monitored if you report to work at 9.30 sharp. If you don't have classes or any meetings, you are free to walk in at any time. Thankfully there are no eagles monitoring your daily routine and passing caustic comments such as "Half-day?" when you walk in 15 minutes late, which is so common in corporates. The path for promotion and increments is clearly laid out without much ambiguity and is not dependent on your last visible performance just prior to the appraisal. In corporates, a lot of subjectivity is involved in promotions. Apple-polishing is known to take people places, literally.

Work-life balance works out well in academics compared to the corporate world. Rarely do we hear academicians requiring 'stress reduction' workshops while this is a common phenomenon in companies. Today, corporates are also realising this and are working towards ensuring a less stressful work environment.

Flexi-timings, work from home option and compulsory vacation time are some of the schemes that have been initiated by corporates. Again, this is more common in start-ups and in IT companies. Manufacturing companies are still catching up on these initiatives. However, the requirement of certain industries and certain specific domains in the industry are such that you need to be on the field and interact with people.

Moreover, the jury is still out on whether these initiatives have a positive impact on the bottom line of the corporate in the long run. It could be counterproductive at times, as some office goers jokingly state that 'work from home' many a times becomes 'work for home.'

Corporate – Academia synergy

There appears to be a visible disconnect between academics and the corporate world. Academics seems to be lagging behind apropos the rapidly transforming corporate landscape. How much of research work is actually being used by corporates? Academia imparts knowledge, has cutting-edge teaching tools and methodologies while corporates have real-time practical issues and are required to come up with innovative on-the-job solutions while working in a complex business environment, while all the time being focused on achieving growth and profitability.

The widening chasm between academia and the corporate world is always a cause for concern. Academic research needs to be made more relevant and specific to the corporates. Is the purpose of academia to solve complex organisational issues? Or to develop an understanding of the processes followed? It should at least instigate a debate or enable a critical reflection on the practices being followed.

"The schism between corporate India and Indian academia seems to be more pronounced than what is experienced in the West, as management research in India has been mostly replicative in nature with limited context specificity. Further, most of the studies are concept-centric rather than problem driven" (Panda and Gupta, 2007).

Academics strive to blend case studies and internships with corporates to give the twin advantage of real-time live examples to their students in addition to theoretical concepts. The increased collaboration between academics and corporates is the need of the hour and the way forward as a synergy between the 2 is important to bridge the gap.

There needs to be 'intellectual arbitrage' between organisations and academia. The concept of 'embedded' students is also gaining traction with students enrolling for part-time research while pursuing a full-time job as part of the collaboration between the company and the institution. This helps in on-the-job training of the students and their employability and their ability to be useful from day one in their debut job increase tremendously.

"In India, a number of initiatives for industry-academia linkages have yielded positive results in research, but these have remained sporadic in nature. India's share in world researchers has persisted at about 2 percent as compared to 20 percent of the USA and China's. The share of research and development (R&D) investments of the USA was 32 percent, of Japan 13 percent and of China 9 percent, while it was only 2.2 percent in India." [Source: UNESCO Institute of Statistics].

"A number of committees have made several recommendations on this issue, significant amongst which were the National Knowledge Commission in 2008, the Kakodkar Committee Report in 2011 on the IITs and the Narayan Murthy Report in 2012. All these reports emphasise the significance of ramping up academia-industry collaboration for augmenting research, innovation, employability and greater productivity, through various measures." [Source: Workshop on Academia – Industry Collaborations March 5th 2013, New Delhi Organised by Ministry of Human Resource Development Government of India]

Why a corporate career is not bad?

Teaching today's students is not a joke. They have their 'Google gurukul' and most of them read up online and pose questions to the professors, not necessarily to clarify their doubts or engage in a discussion. One of the key parameters to rate a professor is her teaching scores, which are dependent on the students rating. Expecting the students to rate the professors rationally is a tall order, especially if the student has not secured desired grades.

In academics, there is a general disdain for corporates and corporate professionals. The general feeling is that they ceaselessly hanker after position, power and money. Well, having a desire for position, power and money is not such a bad thing.

"Corporate jobs can get repetitive" is another lament of the flag bearers of academia. But that is true even for academia. Don't corporates fuel research? Several issues abound, but they are invariably opinions till they are proved by analysis and research of data. Professors too, oftentimes, float the same courses year after year. In addition to teaching, which used to be the mainstay, they are required to do research, publish papers, conduct MDPs, do admin related work, be part of various committees and so on. Some of them are over-burdened with teaching and evaluation load and mundane administrative responsibilities. So, there is an equal amount of stress even in academics.

Corporate guys indulge in subterfuge (of course they do). It's all part and parcel of the corporate game. It's often said that women look for a job and not a career and hence the short-sighted career decisions. Strangely, even though women gravitate towards academics for the freedom, flexibility, love of teaching, etc, academia is also known to be a notoriously 'leaky pipeline' for women. As one moves up the academic ladder, the proportion of women falls off from 40–75% at the time of a PhD conferral to around 10% at the level of full professor.

In corporates, you work hard and get promoted based on your contribution and how strong your boss is. After a certain level, it may not matter as sometimes politics takes over. Whereas in academics, whether you are a great performer or a not so great performer, your increments are uniform and that can be demoralising as well. It's a solitary profession and one needs to have tremendous self-motivation skills. Politics has unfortunately infiltrated the hallowed corridors of academia. The biggest perk of academia is independence of which enough and more has been said. But the flip side to this is that one can become a procrastinator as there is no one to push you. Infighting, jealousy, one-upmanship and so on are no longer spoken about in careless whispers even in academic circles.

People who don't like their job and curse the corporate world at the drop of a hat are missing the point sometimes. There are definitely some things that they must like – it could be the brand, the salary, the environment, anything. They could be hating the boss, but then who has admitted to liking their boss anyway? They could be detesting their peers but these are the disparate parts. They immediately conclude that their jobs suck at the first sign of distress and get ready to take flight

In academics, you are surrounded by some of the best brains as most of them will be PhDs and hence the atmosphere can be intellectually stimulating. Reputed academic institutions are few and maybe, if you are lucky, there may be 1 or 2 noteworthy academic institutions at the place you stay. Hence if you don't like your academic job, getting another one might require relocation. If taking up an academic job was to spend more time with children/elderly parents, a relocation, should it be required, will bring you back to square one. In the corporate world, however, there are a dime a dozen choices and one can easily leave one job and transition smoothly into another without any major upheavals. Industry wins hands down for location flexibility since there are far more industry jobs than tenure-track academic jobs.

In corporates, especially in certain specific industries, at the first sign of trouble, you could be handed a pink slip. Getting another job in troubled times and explaining your pink slip in the previous job to your prospective new employer could really cause heartburns. Recent reports of a popular telecom company closing down major parts of its wireless business which would render several jobless caused a flutter. Losing a job, especially in a mass layoff without any fault of the staff, could be nightmarish for any employee.

In academics, one rarely loses one's job during recession. Although there have been cases, very rarely do professors get fired from academic institutions. And very rarely do professors resign from their jobs except maybe to join a top end B-School from a private college or from a lesser-known B-School. There's no dour-faced boss to suck up to, no subordinates infighting issues which need to be resolved. In academics, there is no 'boss' as such. Wow! A collective hurray can almost be heard. Such a relief! Of late there is a small aberration though. Everybody who is at a level higher than you masquerades as your boss. So there is problem of plenty here.

The constant complaint from the corporate world is that research is out-dated and not in touch with reality. It is not easy to talk of solutions when you have practically not even experienced it. There is some element of truth in this. You begin your research on a seemingly contemporary topic. But by the time you complete your research, the world has moved on and at a rapid pace at that. And you wonder if your findings are relevant and useful by then.

I remember a co-researcher who had never worked in corporates and had no clue about how auditors worked or the challenges in drawing up the financial statements of a company declared that she was planning to work on Earnings Management! I wondered if she would be in a position to carry out meaningful research given that she was far removed from the real world environment. I was tickled pink as I heard her very theoretical talk about auditors and the way they often indulged in accounting jugglery.

In academics, there are classes for 4 to 8 hours per week, time grading assignments and exams, and professional development time where one might attend a seminar or off-campus conference to learn about your field of study, apart from corporate MDPs, interacting with corporates for placements, etc. Add to this the preparatory time for a course, improving the content or delivery of a course and self-research and the actual time spent on these activities goes up enormously.

In addition to this, there are instances of helicopter parents contacting professors directly about their kids' grades and complaining to the department chair and dean. The default reaction from administration is that the professor is at fault. Professors are also penalised if their course grades have too high a percentage of Ds. Institutions are also faced with instances of students arguing and negotiating with the professors for a better grade.

Despite this, several professors express a deep sense of fulfilment and pleasure in the work that they do day in and day out. Although the pay scale for an assistant professor is almost embarrassing, a professor nevertheless has a certain gravitas that is invaluable. However, the prestige associated with the teaching profession has also suffered thanks to the politicisation of higher education.

Some academicians voluntarily choose another path because they want higher pay or more direct engagement with the world than monographs. While we do come across instances of transition from industry to academia, we do not hear much of the reverse. But that could also be due to the fact that transition to academia as a career move is not easily reversible as an academic career does not add to one's career capital as a manager. The academic experience becomes less and less marketable outside of academia.

Everyone has their own priorities and clarifying what you want from your work life will help ensure that you are aiming for careers that will give you job satisfaction.

Benefits of an academic career and of a corporate career

- The level of stability that one enjoys in academia is unique. It gives both peace of mind and freedom to take risks. It provides you with a lot of time to take up research projects. It also gives you the opportunity to act as a bridge. A professor is not bound by any person, dogma, company or ideology. This is in contrast to a company where a person has the mission to contribute to the company's overall value. As a professor, you can learn about different industries and there is a tremendous learning and synthesise that knowledge through research results to the society.
- A professor has the opportunity to give tutorials, develop online courses, write blog posts, teach at local high schools, organise and run workshops and so forth. This is not to say that the same opportunities wouldn't exist in other research positions, but outreach is often not as central to the mission of other jobs as it is to being a professor.

However, some of the benefits of working in industry are:

- Time in the industry is more structured typically because interaction with peers is more predetermined. This leads to higher brainstorming and higher productivity. The real-time problems that you solve, the interactions you have across a cross-domain of professionals, the

result-oriented approach and the risk-taking abilities which get honed are invaluable. The rich and practical industry experience and functional insights that you earn often leads to invitations from top academic institutions to give guest lectures or to become a visiting faculty.
- The decent amount of money you earn ensures that you are able to buy ample downtime and lead a comfortable life without being niggardly. You learn people skills, powers of persuasion, ability to strategize, etc.

Ultimately, the choice between academia and an industry involves many trade-offs, and the best 'fit' often depends on individual preferences and working style. There are certainly drawbacks, and other jobs certainly offer different benefits and perks that jobs in academia do not offer, but the job is far better than one might otherwise be led to believe from recent posts on academic departures.

One can observe that, just as there have been several loud departures from industry, there also remains a very large cadre of extremely happy university professors. However, this could also be due to the fact that top corporate honchos are tracked more seriously and are much more in the limelight than academicians.

Corporates are also hiring PhDs for their R&D cells in a big way. Multinationals and technology firms such as Intel, AMD, Applied Materials, IBM, Bell Labs, Microsoft and Google have also been scouting for PhD scholars for their global research units located in India. Some companies have also launched PhD programmes for their employees in collaboration with IITs/ IISC. These initiatives help the PhD recruits to earn a better pay while working on real-time problems and identifying solutions, thereby making a direct impact.

Corporate Vs Academia is a conundrum with no conclusion on which is an ideal career. There are too many variables and no complex algorithm can solve this. It ultimately depends on the life stage, career aspirations, financial stability, etc.

Chapter 7

Back to Corporate

– by Geeta

"No matter how hard the past, you can always begin"

– Buddha

The concept of *boomerangers*[6] has gained traction in the recent past in a bid to solve the hiring conundrums faced by organisations. From the organisation's point of view, the advantages are manifold. First and foremost, the on boarding costs are minimal, cultural acclimatisation is faster and there is less of a learning curve. The employee is productive from day one (hopefully) and that's a huge saving. Corporates are also faced with a glut of talent. Recruiting and retaining the right talent is an extremely complex process for which no sure shot formula has been discovered till now

As per a 2015 survey by Workplace Trends, 76% of HR professionals said they are more likely to hire 'boomerang employees' now than in the past. This pioneering trend can be attributed to the millennials. The Workplace Trends survey also revealed that almost 50% of the millennials surveyed said they would consider returning to a former employer when compared to just one-third of both Gen X and baby boomers. Social media and alumni networks have also played a crucial role in helping maintain relationships between employers and their former employees.

---

[6] Employees who leave a company and eventually return are called boomerangers.

Chennai-based Avtar I-Win, set up in 2005, was the pioneer in helping women restart their careers. Dr Saundarya Rajesh, Founder of Avtar I-Win, believes that equality often does not work in the gender space in corporates due to the various unique issues that working women face in India. They facilitated the hiring of around 450 women employees for the Future Group way back in 2006.

An overwhelming 91 percent of Indian women want to return to work, similar to the United States (89 percent) and significantly more than Germany (78 percent). Sylvia Ann Hewlett, Founder, Center for Talent Innovation, conducted a study for the past 10 years and released a report (2013) titled *On Ramps and Up Ramps India* and found that the reasons why Indian women quit their jobs are poor work culture (68%), gossip (66%), disparity of remuneration (46%) and lack of recognition (58%). 27% of women surveyed also disliked the type of work they were doing that led to lower job satisfaction. 42% of the women cited lack of opportunity for growth (learning, increased responsibility, etc) as some of the reasons for lower job satisfaction.

Sunil Nayak, CEO, Sodexo India, says that many women who take breaks come back with stronger views and different perspectives.

"Brenda Barnes, CEO of PepsiCo North America, took a 6-year hiatus to focus on her family in Illinois before becoming the CEO of Sara Lee Corp in 2004. Ann Fudge, a prominent African American executive, relinquished her position as president of a $5 billion unit of Kraft Foods to take a 2-year sabbatical; she returned to corporate life as CEO of ad giant Young and Rubicam in 2003 (Brady, 2004; Yang, 2005)."

Employer initiatives to get back ex-employees

As per an article in HBR dated Sept 2016, organisations are focusing on when employees are leaving rather than why employees are leaving. Reasons for employees leaving are standard. According to the article, job hunting activity increases by 6–9% during work anniversaries, by 12% during the birthdays, particularly mid life and by 16% post-school/college reunions. These are the stages where people re-assess, indulge in peer-comparison and introspect about their lives. Organisations are on the lookout for these telltale signs and are indulging in counselling in a bid to retain talent, especially for the star performers.

Several companies have taken initiatives to bring back employees by offering them various facilities. Companies like Infosys, P&G, Accenture, Tata, HCL, Murugappa group and several others have taken steps to address the peculiar problems related to working women by offering benefits such as work from home, flexible working hours, family and medical leave, training, dependent care and support for re-entry, amongst others. Of course, these benefits need to be offered judiciously to selected and talented employees and not to everyone.

Within the Tata group, there are several initiatives, as widely reported by media. They have implemented a group-wide mentoring programme to develop women leaders and the 'Second Career Internship programme (SCIP),' which is a career transition management programme for women professionals who have taken a break of 6 months or more for any reason and wish to re-enter the professional space. There is also a regular reporting and benchmarking of diversity and inclusion metrics. Begun in June 2008, Tata SCIP is a career transition management programme for professionals. It is an intermediary programme aimed at developing alternative talent pools in traditional/non-traditional formats and facilitating career transitions.

As per the Randstad Employer Brand Research, 2017, Google India has been named the most 'attractive employer brand,' for the third year in a row followed by Mercedes-Benz. Salary and employee benefits followed by good work-life balance and job security were the top considerations for workers across all profiles while picking an employer. Not surprisingly, work-life balance has moved up the priority list from fifth to the second rank for employees.

There's a bill before the French government to ban emails out of office hours, and Belgium now protects workers not only from discrimination and harassment but also from burnout. Germany apparently has banned managers from calling their staff beyond office hours. Although this is a welcome move, it is unlikely that it will work in an Indian environment.

How to get back to a corporate job?

Jobs come in all shapes and sizes. You very rarely will land up a job that is up your alley. Most often, you need to design and build around your job to make it engaging and exciting.

Employees need to seek out jobs that will tap their potential and endeavour to find value in the work they do. Realisation needs to dawn that, ultimately, satisfaction or dissatisfaction at work is related to how one approaches the job. One should try to find meaning in their work, or find work that is meaningful to them. A bespoke job is a rare commodity.

Any talk of flexi-time work cannot be concluded without debating about the by now infamous decision by Marissa Mayer of Yahoo who put a kibosh on this practice at her company. Marissa Mayer was apparently of the opinion that collaboration, communication and connection was an important part of office culture and employees need to work side-by-side. Several found it hypocritical as she had stated very clearly early on that her job was not the numero uno priority in her life and that her most significant concerns were God, family and Yahoo – in that order.

"The trick," says Hewlett, "lies in treating flexi-time as a reward rather than entitlement." Hewlett adds, "Offer it to your most talented performers rather than offering it to everyone."

To reclaim your place in a corporate, you need to work towards it. Being updated and networked is so crucial. Ensuring that one has a strong network, is updated and acquires new skills will ensure that the transition back to corporate will be relatively smooth. Talent is in short supply and corporates are keen to identify good workers who have left and persuade them to return.

The other big hurdle that one faces is convincing an employer that you will not take a break again at the drop of a hat. They will look for our commitment and staying power. Many corporates follow the motto of *'Recruit for attitude and train for skills.'* Demonstrating that you are serious about getting back to work will work in your favour.

I have had friends who took a break to take care of their kids and a few months or years into it, they started feeling perfectly useless, restless, taken for granted, etc. It's important to put your feet up for a while but do plan to do something productive else it could lead to depression and a sense of low self-esteem, especially if you are serious about your career.

A cousin of mine who also appeared to be fed up with her 'mundane' job said that she could earn an equal amount of salary by trading in stocks and working less hours and under less stressful conditions. She put in her papers and then followed a series of rounds of negotiations with her boss offering her a higher salary, flexi hours and so on. What is this about corporates that they seem to realise your true worth only when you have put in your papers? She anyway decided to quit. She got more 'me' time and enjoyed her freedom and the flexibility to work. And she was earning as much.

Less than a year down the line, she started getting restless. She missed the interaction with colleagues. She was sleeping more and although she had the time to hit the gym, she was also putting on weight as she was constantly raiding the fridge. The inflow of relatives increased now that she was spending more time at home. Although initially she enjoyed it, she started getting weary with all the talk. During this phase, the comeback calls from her ex-office had commenced and gained momentum. She decided to get back and is now reconciled that this is what she wants… a corporate career with all the warts and freckles…

Why did I get back to my corporate job?

The media is replete with news of people taking a short-term or long-term career break to pursue their passion or give fruition to their dormant desires. Some get back to their corporate careers while some just decide to continue with their new phase of life. Getting back to work after a break is no longer a taboo as in the earlier days. Talking a break from corporate is not the end of life; in fact it's almost become the new normal. Yes, your chances of a coveted position or paycheque could get compromised but then again it depends on the nature of the break. If the break was done to pursue some course which adds value to the current job, chances of losing out on designation and paycheque could be much lower.

Why did I get back to a corporate job? Well, I got a call from my previous employers. They asked me if I would be interested in joining back. I had my initial reservations as this was not necessarily on my agenda. When I decided to take a break, I had wanted to pursue an academic career post my PhD and take on corporate consulting assignments. An academic degree opens up multiple avenues. Further, my sabbatical also made me look at the corporate world through a different prism.

During my break, Ind-AS were introduced, the Companies Act was amended and GST (goods and services tax) was just around the corner. In short, there was an overhaul of several old regulations and it seemed like an exciting time to be in a corporate career as nothing can beat a practical experience. I felt I could always pursue my academic dreams by giving guest lectures or taking up visiting faculty positions and possibly aim for a full-time position a little later.

Getting back to the corporate world after a long hiatus of 4 years could cause anxiety pangs, especially if it is a blurred memory. Several doubts plagued me:

> *What if I had to restart at the bottom of the rung?*
> *Will my break on account of study be given due value and recognition?*
> *Will I be respected or will my return be construed as a sign of weakness?*
> *What if I was taken at a lower designation compared to my other colleagues who were at the same level when I took a break?*

Navigating the corporate world

Are we really dissatisfied or have we been made to feel dissatisfied? A colleague of mine remarked, "How can you do Internal Audit? It's so boring. I wouldn't be caught dead doing audit." Maybe, Internal Audit is not a glamorous profession to be in. Nobody likes you when you are in Internal Audit. People avoid you and keep a safe distance from you. But each to his own. There was this colleague of mine was working for a tax firm filing individual and corporate tax returns. Well, that didn't pique my interest either. How utterly boring, I thought to myself.

One of the biggest lessons in the corporate world is to first be passionate or at least somewhat passionate about your job and be proud of what you are doing. People will always try to prove that the job you are doing is boring, negative, so this and so that in a bid to prove that their job is so much more important, useful, interesting, satisfying and so on. There is a growing tribe which frowns on working in a 'boring desk job.' It's so fashionable to say that "I could never imagine myself in a boring 9 to 5 desk job."

While you are cursing your job, remember there are zillions out there who would give their right hand to be in your place. We are seeking happiness and validation from external sources although it is right within us and we need to take control of our well-being. There is also a popular misconception that happiness will follow success, but author and psychologist Shawn Achor states that 'happiness comes before success.'

Back to corporate was déjà vu for me. It's the workbench culture in corporates that many find so stifling. For people who like structure and discipline, they gravitate towards 9 to 5 jobs. One needs to choose the company of one's choice based on one's list of priorities to feel energised enough to go to work on a Monday morning. Not everyone can chuck their job and decide to become an entrepreneur.

The media needs to take a large share of the blame in portraying entrepreneurs as the next big thing that happened after the internet. A ring of romance and glamour has been attached to entrepreneurship. One needs to factor in that as an employee, you work for the company, but as an entrepreneur, you need to work for your employees. Organisational navigation is not for the faint-hearted. It teaches you several survival skills, which may appear to be a waste of time for most but are essential.

One of my close friends who had initial hiccups in his career due to a combo of bad luck and bad choices, but bounced back to scale the peak, summarises the proper way to go about your corporate career. He says that one could shift jobs in the first 10 years of one's career to get a sense and feel of what one really wants. Thereafter one should select a job and be with it through thick and thin at least for the next 10 years. Thereafter, if required, one could make that one final/last career shift and retire from that company.

Sounds so simple and doable, right? It's not that simple in practice though one should always try. It's also extremely important to have a mentor to guide you through the initial years of your corporate career. Unfortunately, most of us never have one and underestimate the need for one.

Now I am back to the rough and tumble corporate grind. Have things changed much? Yes and no. When I walked in at 9.25 am to the office on the first day after the long hiatus, it seemed a bit scary. I noticed that my co-workers and my team members were walking in from 9.40 till 10. And it wasn't even a hurried *the feeling a tad guilty for walking in late* kind of a walk. It was a confident walk with the head held high and a smile without the slightest trace of guilt.

I told myself that it was one of those days and it must surely be an aberration. When it continued, it rankled. I quickly summoned the team and made it amply clear that office timings were sacrosanct and they had to be adhered to under any circumstances and that late-comings could be an exception and not the rule. They all nodded solemnly and still continued to do as per their bidding.

The reasons of course varied from not well, woke up late, vehicle puncture, traffic jam, etc., which were uttered without batting an eyelid. For women, there were additional reasons such as MIL not keeping well, child not well, gynac issues and so on which ensured that the male boss had no choice but to shut his mouth. As per their opinion, these were perfectly justified.

These are perfectly acceptable excuses in the Indian context. Corporates have often accused women of expecting unreasonable allowances. I wonder if it's to do with the culture. Some would cheekily sneak in a "But madam, we don't leave by 5.30 in the evening." To which I very sternly told him what my earlier boss had told one of my colleagues who was a serial late-comer, "Coming early is my prerogative; going late is yours."

Nothing much has changed since then. Suddenly one week, I found that 2 of them were in office even before 9.30 am and I was pleased as a punch. Only later did I realise that they were attending some classes in the morning and hence were early to office. Welcome to the millenial world!

HR is grappling with millennials who set their own rules and almost appear irreverent. Unable to tackle this issue and find solutions, they have tactfully outsourced discipline and other related admin matters to the heads of the respective departments. Millennials represent the affluent generation that grew up with notions of fun and frolic as their central activity and expect this lifestyle to percolate in their workforce as well.

Today, many millennials expect beanbags, free lunch, flash dance and other similar perks as part of the corporate package. Visuals of employees lounging in a hammock with earphones plugged in and laptops perched on their knees while working are not an unthinkable proposition anymore, especially in some IT companies and start-ups.

Gen-Y has tremendous attitude and chutzpah. They are not willing to be shackled by official timings, formal wear, etiquette, etc. It is a common sight to watch these youngsters casually sauntering in the office well past the office opening hours with their earphones on.

Now it's back to the concrete world. I hope to blend the theoretical world with the practical world. Being in Audit, one of the pillars of corporate governance, it gives me first-hand insight into the working of the Audit Committee (AC). The time spent by the AC in deliberating the audit issues, the constitution of the AC, the number of meetings held, percentage attendance of the AC members, etc, the common variables used in regression on Audit Committee related studies are all observed by me at close quarters.

Of course, cut-throat competition is back. One-upmanship and politics are back. Office politics is an inescapable part of working life, and it isn't optional. In most corporates, the turf is demarcated subtly sometimes and clearly sometimes. Office turf wars are not uncommon.

If the reason for moving away from corporate is all of these and lack of growth, opportunities, bad boss, try working on these and find solutions or alternatives. Giving up or running away is not the solution. If not in office, in our day-to-day life, we will face similar problems. We are neither living in a utopian world nor can we be an ostrich.

Maybe one needs to give a hard look at one's career goals or realign them. A job might be stressful, but being without a job can also cause acute stress for some. The American Psychological Association reported in early 2017 that Americans were reporting more stress than ever owing to politics, the speed of change and uncertainty in the world. Some of us have this self-righteousness of how could he (read boss, co-worker) do this to me? How could he play such double games with me? How could he this and how could he that? Well, we need to accept that the world abounds with such people who have their own agenda and play nasty games. So, deal with it. Quitting need not always be the solution though most throw in their hat at the slightest sign of disturbance.

Yes, toxic bosses do abound – 'boss-hole' as per the moniker bestowed by millennials on such people. Try understanding his reasons and work around them. However, should the boss cripple initiative, be overly critical, micro-manage, indulge in verbal abuse, set unrealistic targets, etc., then it's time to get a transfer within the company or outside the company.

Remember that bad bosses do not always last. In one my previous companies, my boss and I didn't see eye to eye. Despite trying my best to meet his expectations and buy some peace, it didn't work. I put in my papers. Less than a month later, my boss too quit. If only I had paid some heed to the office grapevine, I would have got to know about his plans and could have put up with him for just a month more. To be fair not all bosses are the frankensteins that we make them out to be. There are several lessons to be learnt from them but we have been fed with such horror stories of these monster bosses that we turn blind and deaf.

Having both passion and skill for a particular job is ideal. Unfortunately, most of us have the passion for A and skill for B. Sometimes decades get wasted in trying to figure out what one really wants. One keeps searching for this ultimate job that sometimes doesn't exist or is difficult to get. Oftentimes we are ourselves not sure of what we really want. Many choose the next best option of continuing with one's job, however dull or boring it may be, as one needs to keep the fire burning. One then pursues one's true passion on the sidelines.

One of the most famous cases in American culture is that of Charles Ives, the composer, whose music is highly respected and often performed by symphony orchestras. He spent most of his life working for the Hartford Insurance Company in Connecticut and wrote music on his own time. Money does not buy happiness – but it does allow you to be miserable in comfort.

Comparisons are odious. A friend or colleague might be earning much more than you and you feel shortchanged. Chances are that s/he is burning the midnight oil frequently, working without breaks, travelling incessantly, is overloaded, etc. You are probably earning less but in a more satisfying job with an inspiring boss or a more reputed company.

Evaluate and compare after considering all the parameters, not just the monetary aspect. You probably fare much better and need to stop whining. One needs to go through this learning curve. Manufacturing companies are wont to paying less when compared to an IT company, MNC company or consulting firm. Au contraire, in IT companies, consultancy companies, ad agencies, etc., which are client-driven and which are guided by stiff deadlines, working way beyond the office hours is the norm rather than an exception. Working late into the night, sleepless nights, client calls at odd hours, especially if working for clients in a different time zone, is part of the job.

Given the crazy hours one ends up spending at office, one needs to have decent coworkers. After all, you will spend more time with them than your parents or children. Work is contagious. Most people walk around with long faces; if they were a little longer they would touch the ground. Why don't we see more happy faces at work? Monday blues hits most employees – several look like something the cat dragged in.

Is job satisfaction so difficult to attain? What is the solution to unhappiness at work? Unfortunately, it's complex. On the employers' side, management needs to do a better job of selecting and placing workers in jobs that are a good fit. Good leadership involves challenging workers and recognising employees for the good work they do. Building a workplace culture that is positive and engages employees is important.

I too had already switched more than half a dozen jobs in search of that dream job prior to taking a break. "What do you exactly want?" my father would ask exasperatedly, repeatedly. I wish I knew. I just want to enjoy my journey I guess. At least I thought so. I wasn't sure.

One needs to stop looking at external sources for satisfaction and gratification. You need to find that job which meets your aspirations and imagination. While getting an 'ideal' job is the ideal situation, most of us are not in that coveted club. One then needs to do the second best thing. Seek self-satisfaction. Seek satisfaction in whatever you are doing and do it to your best ability. Basically, give it your best shot.

We make the cardinal mistake of waiting for external sources such as the corporate environment, boss, designations to motivate us. We need to really work on self-motivation and constantly up the bar. We need to be the custodians of our own happiness. The one question we need to pose to ourselves is that are we working for food, housing, clothing or for passion and fulfilment?

Don't always believe people who go on and on about how they have this perfect job, how they are doing exactly what they wanted to do in life and so on. There are several who flourish on creating this hype on how they have landed this picture-perfect job. Take these stories with a pinch of salt. I have come across several such people who quit barely couple of years after they tom-tommed about how wonderful their jobs were. No one knows the inner story – the real story.

There will be some who would have stuck to a job for several years. It could be that they have met their aspirations and requirements in the job, not necessarily loving it but it's not bad either. It could also be a case of resilience, zero risk-taking or reconciliation.

People with highly valued academic credentials do not necessarily have a successful corporate career. I have always wondered about this dichotomy. A good qualification helps to get an entry into a reputed organisation, but thereafter it is a combination of smart work, networking and hard work with dollops of luck. People management, an extremely important skill, is not taught in colleges. Organisation navigation is another skill which needs to be acquired in a jiffy on the job. The need to observe more and listen more instead of talking is another trait which needs to be cultivated. Does additional qualification bring about more wisdom, insights and maturity or does it make one arrogant?

Some feel extremely claustrophobic in their work environment. We probably have unreasonable expectations from our employer. In today's world of instant gratification, people are ready to throw the hat at the slightest provocation. They quit their job in a huff or a whim and take up another only to encounter a different set of problems, or worse, a similar set of problems. Some of us live in this utopian world where everything should be picture-perfect. We need to own up and be ready to face the harsh realities of life, chin up.

Workplace irritants will be plenty and its up to us to rise above the mundane and seek a larger vision/goal. We tend to get embroiled in the sob stories of our co-workers and this pulls us down and gets us demotivated. Avoid the chronic cribber. Channelizing one's energy into productive things and being wise enough to acknowledge that it's not possible to have it all or do it all will go a long way in proving one's lifestyle. There are only 24 hours in a day, of which work takes away more than 10 hours, 7 hours go towards sleep which leaves us with only 7 hours in which we are to bathe, cook, eat, spend time with parents/children, shop and be entertained. But unfortunately, most of us have a line-up of desires, which are not possible to accomplish as there is no time for all of it. This unnecessarily causes us stress. Some of these activities itself can turn into a source of stress.

On paper the working hours in any typical Indian firm is 9.30 to 5.30. Nobody leaves at 5.30, except for a few secretaries. Even if you have done your task for the day, you don't leave at 5.30 unless you want to become the butt of caustic remarks. So you hang in there and prepare to leave any time after 6.30. Clocking at least an hour post the end of business hours is looked upon with favour at corporates. You at least should not aspire to leave before your boss. It's ok if you pack up the next minute after your boss leaves but not before him/her. And if you leave after your boss, make sure you don't let this golden opportunity slip by. Write a note on the work that you were doing or conjure up something and sign off with a flourish at the bottom stating 20 hrs or 21 hrs. Your boss will be pleased as punch. Most employees clock in 50 hours per week. Throw in a smartphone and this number rises exponentially. In effect, the number of hours we are working and thinking of work is mind-boggling.

Women matter

India Inc. is still a male-dominated arena and is expected to continue to be one for a long, long time. Despite this, the fact that some Indian women now occupy prominent positions and their rightful place in the corporate world bears testimony to their perseverance, patience and courage. Their *Sitzfleisch* is commendable and needs to be recognised. According to the WEF, overall Global Gender Gap Index ranking of the World Economic Forum (WEF), Women around the globe may have to wait for more than 2 centuries to achieve equality in the workplace.

Do women promote women? There have been several reports which talk about the oft-debated notion of a 'Queen Bee' syndrome, which argues that women who have made it to senior positions actively seek to boycott and exclude other women from promotions into senior management positions.

Today with flexible corporate structures, enabling technologies and changing dynamics in marriage, women are in a position to climb the rungs of the corporate ladder without necessarily sacrificing their personal life roles. Several avenues have opened up for women giving them options, especially in the IT, ITES sector and some MNCs. Several work–family measures in Indian organisations are surprisingly found in the public sector. Hence, women can make a conscious call on which career/industry to pursue given their circumstances.

Women face barriers, some real and some imaginary. Yes, much has been made about the glass ceiling and it does exist, in some places rather blatantly and in some in a disguised manner. This results in women dropping off from their career and going off the radar.

With major corporates buying-in to the negative stereotype of women in senior management is not helping the case either. This further aggravates the thin bandwidth/already existing shortage of women in top management cadre. Women too have used this as an excuse for not progressing in their careers.

While corporates are waking up to the need of gender diversity, several are reluctant to appoint women to key managerial positions or critical functions for fear of a vacuum being created or interruptions caused due to their premature exit. Gender stereotyping does exist. Women role models were few and hence there was no benchmark for me, when I kick-started my career. There were only a handful of women in the senior management position as a result of which I didn't have a mentor to advise and encourage me. Further, although some women had fancy positions, there was no empowerment. Several like me learnt the ropes the hard way and had to struggle to breach and reach the senior management band.

Of course there are several factors that guide and control one's career trajectory to the top position. One should of course work towards rising higher in one's chosen field and improve the probability of success and improve one's chances. As per a 2012 HBR article, "In this tough economy and ever-changing world, it is more important than ever to smartly evaluate each step in your career."

Researchers often deliberate about 'dominance penalty' – the way our culture rewards and promotes men for acting dominantly, but silently penalises women for doing the same. This forces women to make a choice and face a compromise between perceived competence and being liked by their colleagues. Further, women are judged by the means adopted to accomplish a task while a man is judged by the end results or 'deliverable,' means be damned. Men have generally channelled their leadership method to focus on the task, while women have done so to focus on people or the relationship.

Although several attempts have been made by corporates to increase the number of women in a bid to bring about diversity, one prominent step being the mandatory requirement to appoint a woman director on the Board, many opine that this is just tokenism. Professor Boris Groysberg of Harvard Business School said in 2013 that "Diversity is about counting the numbers. Inclusiveness is about making the numbers count." Affirmative action from some corporates is initially expected to help draw the attention to this issue and expected to go a long way.

Should you decide to leave a job, it's important to end on good terms and maintain a cordial relationship with your employer, especially since you may find yourself wanting to come back one day. On the other hand, given the drying talent pools, the organisation is likely to reach out to you and offer you a job to get back, possibly at a higher position/designation.

Ursula Burns, the woman who rose from an intern to the top position of CEO of Xerox, has this to say to ambitious women who want to achieve all their career goals: "Find a good, older husband. Achieving women believe they have to be outstanding every single day at being a parent, spouse and contributor in your work environment," she told ASME. "If you are trying to do that, you are going to crash and burn and very likely not be outstanding at any of it."

One of my colleagues in one of my previous jobs was very clear that money was his biggest driving force. He wanted a job that would pay him the sky. He was aggressive and expected a promotion every other year. He had clarity and that is extremely important to not lose focus from the goal.

Having worked in half a dozen companies, I can say this now on hindsight that there is no such thing as a blockbuster job. You need to know that everything will rarely pan out the way you anticipate. You need to arrive at your own list of negotiable and non-negotiable aspects.

Some of the things women could do to enhance their career

- Put your hand up for stretch assignments where you take on extra work. Women over analyse the challenge and shy away from work for fear of failure or the extra strain it is likely to cause on their personal life.
- Push yourself out of your comfort zone.
- Keep yourselves updated, keep pace with industry and technological trends and cultivate new skills in the relevant field of work.
- Women also need to be heard and hence they need to speak up at meetings. According to a study published in HBR in 2014, if and when women do speak up at meetings, they apologise repeatedly and allow themselves to be interrupted.
- Be present on social/professional networking sites like Facebook/ LinkedIn. Networking which is the current key to success and visibility doesn't come naturally to women as they perceive it to be inauthentic and too transactional.
- Making small changes in your job, like collaborating with colleagues or mentoring a junior employee, can make your work feel more meaningful.
- Pick and choose a boss/ mentor, not a company.
- Make your boss look good, always.
- Develop a vision for yourself, for your life.
- Experience and visibility are necessary for advancement to senior leadership. Work on them.
- You need to figure out how to add value outside of your role.
- As time progresses, the technical skills that we were so proud of start to matter less and less. Man management and how we interact with people start to matter a lot more. Develop these skills.
- Understand your innate strengths and weaknesses and develop insights into your interests and dislikes, your passion and your skills. This will help you to play to your strengths. This will help you to push yourself in the right direction. Not all of us are designed to become CEOs.
- Remember that real success comes less from controlling people that report to you and more from the ability to align stakeholders who surround you.

- Identify a mentor from who it is extremely important to learn, get feedback and insights.
- Try to be around successful people in your respective field. The learning will be immense and invaluable.
- If you're early in your career and they give you a choice between a great mentor or higher pay, opt for the mentor every time. And don't even think about leaving that mentor until your learning curve peaks.
- You need to know how to navigate the world of office politics.
- You need to figure out what your company needs, and give it to them.
- Some of us expect too much of hand holding which doesn't normally take place. Train yourself to be a self-starter and be self-motivated.
- No job is objectively good or bad. It's what you make of it. We need to retrofit our careers.
- To rise up the ladder and get promoted, apart from your boss putting up your case, your performance, etc it's your attitude in working one level above your current level which plays a key role in your elevation.
- When you hate your job but continue to be in that state without doing anything, it only adds to stress and anxiety and causes health problems.

What corporates need to do

While many organisations have been able to improve their policies related to maternity leave and a few have invested in building some infrastructure for daycare for children of employees, very few have found answers for women leaving work later in their careers for taking care of elders. Since the percentage of women quitting their jobs mid-way is higher on account of geriatric care rather than paediatric care, the onus is on the corporates to take initiatives for this. Probably a daycare for aged parents of employees!

Employees have often complained of 'meeting fatigue'. It is not an uncommon sight to observe people huddled together discussing aplenty over copious cups of caffeine and PPTs. Most offices are meeting intensive, so much so that offices sometimes bear a deserted look what with most employees locked in meeting rooms. Some come out of a meeting only to pop into another meeting. It's not clear how many are actually invested in a meeting, given the numerous interruptions, non-stop phone calls, etc. Corporates need to work towards creating a culture of fewer and more focused meetings and look for alternate formats to the meetings.

Corporates need to optimise performance not attendance. They need to focus on outcome not output. While facetime is required in certain kinds of jobs, flexi-timings, work from home options, part-time employment, extended paediatric/geriatric care furloughs, etc., could be explored and provided as a reward to deserving employees.

Robust mechanisms should be put in place to ensure that constant and on-the-job feedback is provided to employees to prevent nasty shocks during annual appraisal.

There has been a shift by corporates who are focused on better earnings and maximising shareholder's wealth rather than employee welfare. In a bid to appease stakeholders, stringent cutbacks on medical benefits, health insurance, salary hikes, investment in employee training, etc have been resorted to which has piqued many deserving employees.

Conclusion

The New Beginning...

Books on career changes have flooded the market in recent times. But this one hopefully has provided some specific perspectives on *corporate and academia* specifically as it draws heavily on the personal experiences of the authors. It has also tried to dwell on the important aspect of *how to deal with career breaks* in detail.

The Indian corporate landscape has seen a lot of dynamics in the recent decades. Thanks to globalisation and information technology upsurge, opportunities in many sectors have exploded. And there is a lot of variety even in terms of jobs being in different stages of the business cycle – introduction, growth, maturity, etc. Although the format of a corporate career has changed to some extent with options such as part-time, flexi-timings, work from home being offered by various corporates, it is still a high pressure, late working hours, little time for personal life-kind of a format, especially in the private sector.

Corporates have woken up to this reality and are actively taking initiatives and implementing different options with a view to retaining good talent, which is in short supply in the market. There have been several who have straddled this world and have managed to find a balance between work and home and have managed it successfully. For some, working in a corporate, dealing with real-time problems, albeit with pressure still provides an adrenaline rush.

While it does hold a great appeal to a working professional to start one's career journey with, as he/she gets into middle life, the demands of the job have high personal consequences. And this is where the topic of a career shift is thought about by several as it becomes relevant at mid life. Of course if one is the primary breadwinner, the decision may be different but otherwise there is a serious evaluation that an individual undergoes in terms of figuring out which career would help them balance domestic and work responsibilities. For such people, public sector comparatively facilitates a better work-life balance.

Academics is one such option. There may be many others, such as self-employment, but this one has been covered in detail, as our journey has been in that. We are not in the least suggesting that academics is a default career choice! But the dynamics and the nature of it probably makes it suitable to pace it around a more holistic life – personally and professionally in the Indian context, especially for women contemplating a mid life career shift, for whom money is not a big issue and who are passionate about teaching. Of course, some women transition this troubled phase by reinventing themselves successfully and find a higher meaning in whatever they are doing. Some women overcome their anxieties, frustrations and come out trumps in their corporate careers as well.

However, to answer a question on why do a PhD when one doesn't necessarily or eventually become a professor, the answer is that the motivations, desires vary from person to person. Doing a PhD need not necessarily culminate in an academic career. There are several demands from Big 4 firms and corporates for PhDs especially for data analytics and Financial Modelling. IT companies have also been ramping up their PhD recruits for their research labs. Several people train for marathons, triathalons and undergo gruelling training sessions although there is no desire to turn into full-time professional athletes. It just gives some an inexplicable high to push themselves out of their comfort zones and aim higher.

We have explored all of these in the book. We envision that there is a still a lot of intervention work is required in this area. As far as careers for women go, a lot more needs to be done in terms of facilitating career breaks, working out sabbaticals, arriving at flexible work hours etc. in the Indian context. Work-life balance is now a vital driver of career choices and therefore it is an important consideration for organisations. Very few reliable databases are available and that indicates the amount of research that needs to be done. There are just a handful of organisations and consultants in this domain who provide insights and clarity on how to go about this space of mid life career choices.

And there are innumerable talented women out there who simply give up working because there are unable to get a mentor to help chase their dreams as well as fulfil their domestic responsibilities. This can also range from getting a domestic help or even just get access to counselling to make them aware of how to go about this critical life stage, without renouncing their professional identity. And in this last step is where we feel we can make a difference.

A word of caution – be aware of the possibilities and pitfalls of the decision. The path is fraught with considerable challenges, some known but mostly unknown. We have tried to share our decision-making process, our journey, our struggles, our learnings which we hope will be of immense value to you. Is there any right method? Is there a better method? We are sure there is…we just need to discover it…

We are hoping that in the process of our journey, we have upgraded from version 1.0 to version 2.0. Hemingway's wise words come to our mind, "It is good to have an end to journey towards; but it is the journey that matters, in the end."

We are unable to see a future when work life will become less important. With technology intervention and automation increase, people are spending less and less time at home. Therefore doing something personally meaningful can happen only if we are engaged in something just beyond our homes. In fact we don't put it beyond us to conceive of another book titled 'Late life career choices' soon! With the longevity of human race acquiring a new high, *we owe it to life itself to come up with work ideas that will leave this world a better place, we owe it to ourselves.*

Moving forward, we plan to conduct workshops to reach out to those women who want to do this balancing act. We will make them realise that theirs is a not a unique problem and that they do not need to go through it alone. They can meet and network with similar minded people who have travelled this path earlier and have come out of it successfully. We can connect them to organisations that may be able to find opportunities for them based on their current situation. As stated earlier, women's place in the workforce is crucial and it is important that they work together as a society to ensure that their identity is intact as both a personal family contributor as well as a working professional.

Till then, do write to us with your feedback on this book. We will meet you in your city and have a personal interaction soon.

Much love

Rajeshwari and Geeta.

Appendix 1

Responses have been collated from women going through career transition from corporate to academia and vice versa. They have spent close to 10–35 years in corporate life.

1. Is the mid-career shift decision for men and women very different?

"It is different as the challenges faced by both are different with respect to expectations. However progressive a society is, the role of women and men are different."

"The context of marriage defines roles differently in most cases for men and women. There are challenges of location/geographical mobility and finding a support system. In fact the personal dilemma is higher when situations warrant more attention due to childcare. All these make it increasingly difficult to maintain work-life balance in corporate life. The so called 'breaks' or 'shifts' that women make are not heard of, as they are in the case of men."

2. What is the right age for women to consider this shift?

The right time to consider a shift is more life stage dependent rather than age dependent. I would say closer to 40, as a certain amount of emotional maturity is required for this decision. I think it is age dependent based on the number of years of experience already achieved. The shift can happen when the family needs more attention.

3. Are certain careers more suited for women?

"Career choices are more personality dependent rather than gender. Women prefer careers where there is flexibility and where careers can be resumed from where they left off."

"Stereotyping is now losing appeal. Women are breaking many barriers."

"Some say quality of time spent with children and family is more important than the quantity of time, but it is not true. Our mere presence at home makes a lot of difference to children and elders in the family."

"Any job that allows you to be back home between 5 pm to 6 pm and which doesn't require your time on a regular basis after 6 pm is the one that suits women. I believe that the strength of the women is in handling the family well and establishing the bond between family members and men will not be able to replace women completely."

"I wouldn't say careers are gender specific, but nurturing, mentoring and training come more easily to women."

"It only depends on the woman and their attitude and personality. All careers are suitable to all. However, support systems are required for both men and women. Men are more likely to have wives at home than women! So if support systems can be established then no career is less suited for a woman."

4. What are the organisational interventions possible, both from corporate and academic?

"The organisational interventions could include child care facilities, senior woman mentors, counselling services, one hour per day for personal work, flexible working for some years, second career options, wok from home, etc."

"Having to work with people at least 10 years younger than you when you come back to your career is a challenge, especially because today's youth do not always respect age and may think of you as not so smart as them because you are at the same place but older. So organisations can handle this by offering some refresher courses to assess if the returning employee is capable of handling higher responsibilities when she comes back."

"(Academic) Institutions can promote more visiting and guest faculty to provide an avenue for working professionals to test out academic interests. More industry academia interactions to improve education content and focus can bring in more of industry into academia. A quota for women can be explored to improve the number of women in such categories."

5. What are the governmental interventions possible?

"Governmental interventions such as long leave for maternity and/or paternity would be very helpful. If the government mandates the above for all private companies too, in addition to providing them for government employees, it would greatly help."

"However, long leave for maternity has unintended consequences of companies hesitating to take women at that stage. If you can't settle your life in 3 months it's difficult to do so in 6 months."

"UGC and other academic bodies should consider people moving from corporate to academics with a more balanced view. One may be starting a career in academics at 40, but currently the number of years in corporate has no weightage or bearing on the academic career. Professionally speaking, such experts bring a lot more to the table. However for purposes of career advancement and recognition the laws still seem to be archaic and do not value this experience."

"With the dearth of teachers and faculty, more options for people wanting only to be associated with teaching/research should be identified. Such people can bring in fresh perspectives from the corporate world. A blend of consulting and research would help to elevate the standard of education. Alternate models of teaching resource development should be identified."

"Conducive regulatory framework – maternity & paternity leave, incentives to organisations having better women employee ratio, enforcement of POSH in true spirit, etc will help."

6. How do you perceive your currently chosen academic/corporate career?

"Academic career is still seemingly insulated from reality. Many perceive the shift as taking the easy way out. Meritocracy is underrated in this field, which needs to change."

"Academia as per me is easier to handle because:

- It gives you greater independence to do your own thing at your defined pace.
- Allows you greater flexibility.
- You are better respected for the effort you put in and not only just the output."

"While working in academics one can experience 2 major benefits – 1. Life is predictable and therefore the daily timings are predictable. One can plan to be involved in children's activities and be more or less a 'stay at home' mom with a few hours of work. 2. There is not much travel involved so there is less or no dependence on others for personal stuff. One is pretty much able to manage both worlds well.

I signed on to my current corporate job with the same specifications – I leave in the afternoons, and I do not travel. However over the last 3 and a half years that I have been here, there have been numerous occasions where I have had to stay full day and travel is an expected part of my job. I still have a lot of flexibility because of my afternoons being off (more or less) but I am a working mom now with a decent amount of time at home.

The biggest problem in making the shift from full-time corporate to half time corporate or academic is the huge financial loss. My salary in academics was 80% less than in corporate. And my half time corporate job gives me 50% less than what a full-time job would fetch me."

7. Please write any other issue that you may feel is relevant to this topic.

"I think it may be a little easier for unmarried women to make this shift simply because their responsibilities are usually lesser and therefore they can take the risk more easily.

On the other hand, the single woman will have to look after aged parents if not young children and that can be more taxing. In India, men are stereotyped to be the main bread winner of the family and they cannot afford to take a break in their career or shift their career easily. The income from women is considered as a bonus in most families. So, they can take a break and go for a mid-career shift.

Also, if the question is specific to shifting to academics, men also consider the remuneration as a factor. Since generally academic institutes do not pay as much as industry, men may not prefer it much, while for women, they are fine with it as they are able to maintain a decent work-life balance in academics.

I think people in academics are generally less stressed and happier since they are working for the joy of the work rather than the salary."

"I was in corporate in IT industry for 14 years until my son was 6 years old. The job demanded me to stay till late night in office and sometimes I used to even stay back overnight in office. Even when I was at home, I had to attend to client calls anytime, irrespective of it being early in the morning or late in the evening. My personal time with the child and the family was compromised. But since the child was not in school yet and I had my parents/ in-laws supporting me, I was able to manage until the child was 6 years old. After that, I realised that my child needed more of my attention. I decided that this kind of job cannot continue for another 25 years. I knew that after a few years, though my child would be an adult, I will have elders at home who need to be taken care of. I therefore wanted to shift to a job in which I don't need to compromise on my personal life.

Banking, academics and working part-time were some options I explored. Academics excited me more but that required investment of few years for a post graduate degree and a PhD. I was ready to do that and so I am in academics now. Now, I am able to spend the evenings with my family and except for very few days in a year, the weekends are completely for the family and myself. I am able to help my son too in his studies. I am sure this would not have been possible if I had continued in corporate. There is no stress in my mind when I am at home which was not the case was during my corporate days."

Appendix 2

A Sample Course Outline: 'New Product Development.'

Course description and objective

New products are an integral part of any business's survival and growth strategy. Despite their importance, the success rates are alarmingly low across industries. Though New Product Development (NPD) is a cross-functional effort, more often than not, the Marketing function plays a lead role in the same.

This 20 session course on *Management of NPD and Introduction* is aimed at familiarising students with the process of NPD right from the ideation stage till the final market launch stage. Aspects such as NPD metrics, NPD success factors, role of market research in NPD are also covered during the course.

A cross industry perspective will be provided wherever relevant.

Pedagogy

Will be a combination of class lectures, video shows, case discussions and book reviews. Students will also be given group assignments and opportunities to present their work in class. Pre-reading material will be a part of the lesson plan booklet or sent as a soft copy.

There will be one field work project that will enable students to put in practice what they have been taught as a part of their curriculum.

Reading material

Recommended text book

> "Winning at New Products"
>
> – *Robert Cooper*

Reference text books

1. Innovation and NPD – PAUL TROTT
2. New Products Management – MERLE CRAWFORD
3. Jugaad innovation – a frugal and flexible approach – 'NAVIRADJOU, JAIDEEP PRABHU& SIMONE AHUJA'
4. New Product Management – R K SRIVASTAV
5. Crossing the chasm – Robert Moore

Book review

> Making Breakthrough Innovation Happen
>
> – *'Porus Munshi'*

Evaluation scheme

Course evaluation will be an equal combination of continuous assessment and final end-examination. The continuous assessment will comprise surprise quizzes, field project work presentation and class assignments. End examination will be in written format for a duration of 3 hours and will test the students' understanding of the various concepts in NPD and their application through a business case analysis.

Marks allocation

1. Continuous assessment – 65%
   - Quiz – Individual – 15%
   - Field work presentation – Group – 30%

- Assignment – Group – 10%
- Class participation – Individual –10%
2. Final end examination – Individual – 35%

Learning objectives

Students will learn how to put in place a new product process for an organisation if it does not exist or will be able to evaluate the existing process and make changes if required. They will use critical thinking, risk management, analytical and decision-making skills while doing this. The key aspect that will be evaluated here is: *Ability to convert an idea into a commercial new product that is potentially viable in the market place.* This will be evaluated through a field project where they will study NPD process in a company and analyse their NPD metrics. Class assignments and tests will also help in the evaluation.

Group project

Identify one company, understand their existing new product process in detail and recommend areas of improvement. Also identify 2 ways in which they measure their new product success. A group size of 5–6 is recommended.

In addition to class presentations, there will be an assessment based on questions to the group as well as a word document submission.

Detailed session schedule (1.5 Hours per session – total 20 sessions)

Session 1, 2 Topics – Lesson Plan discussion – Definition of New Product and Classification of the same – Importance of New Products in business – Cross industry perspective Reading – Brun, E, and Gelswik, M. Classification of ambiguity in NPD Projects. European Journal of Innovation Management. Videos – Types of ads – Innovation at P@G
Session 3 Topics – Innovation vs creativity vs new product – New product management in an organisation – challenges/ stakeholders – Organisational structures and cross-functional teams Reading – Dwyer, L and Miller. R. 'Organisation Environment – New Product process activities and project outcomes.' Journal of Product Innovation and Management – Dwyer, M and Ledwidth, A *'Determinants of new product performance in small firms.'* International Journal of Entrepreneurial Behaviour and Research Videos – Creating an Innovative mindset (Vijay Govindarajan) – P@G Olay innovation – Making Innovation effective by organisation culture Case – 3M Company-B2B

Session 4, 5

Topics
- Steps in NPD-Description
- NPD Models and Framework – Stage Gate process

Reading
- Succeeding at new products the P@G Way
- How to implement the Stage Gate process in your company-

Video
- Successful NPD in 5 steps

Case
- Pharma Industry

Session 6

Topics
- PIC – Product Innovation charter
- Product protocol
- Product design

Reading
- Controlling prototype development through risk analysis – Richard Baskerville

Videos
- NPD Product Innovation charter
- Co creation

Case
- LEGO – Child's play?
- GSM vs CDMA Product design – Mobile industry

Session 7, 8

Topics
- Market research and its role in NPD
- Testing new product/ new concept-Conjoint Analysis
- Defining action standards for go/ no go decisions

Reading
- Concept testing – an appropriate approach – Bill Luso

Videos
- Ethnography research
- Disruptive Innovation

Caselet
- Nokia
- Pepsi Kona

Session 9, 10

Topics
- Decision to commercialise
- Business analysis
- Sales forecast

Reading
- Simon, R. 'NPD and forecasting challenges. The Journal of Business forecasting.'

Videos
- Sales forecasting at FORD EDGE (15 Min)
- Innovation challenges in emerging markets

Case
- Toyota PRIUS-Automotive industry NPD

Session 11, 12

Topics
- Pricing a new product

Reading
- Pricing and the psychology of consumption – John Gourville and Dilip Soman

Video
- Making of Tata NANO

Case
- Clinic Plus pricing

Session 13

Topics
- Launch Management
- Contingency planning
- Market information systems
- Launch audit

Reading
- Panwar, J.S and Bapat. D. 'New Product Launch Strategies, Insights from Distributor's Survey.' South Asian Journal of Management.

Videos
- Launching a new product
- Innovate like Google

Case
- CAVINKARE – Challengers taking on Giants
- SPINVOX – Launching a technology product

Session 14

Topics
- New product adoption
- Technology product marketing
- Global Take off for new products

Reading
- Langley, J.D and Pals, N. *'Adoption of behaviour: Predicting success for major innovations.'* European Journal of Innovation Management
- 'How to reduce market penetration cycle times' – Thomas Robertson

Videos
- Apple Innovation
- Product categories versus Technology Innovation-Stanford
- How early adopters reach when mass marketed (4: 34 min)

Case
- NOVATIUM – Computing Technology

Session 15

Topics
- Measuring new product process effectiveness
- Defining metrics across NPD steps
- NPD Productivity
- Innovative intensity of an organisation

Reading
- 'NPD Measurement'-Bhuiyan
- National Knowledge Commission 2007

Video
- Measuring /metrics for creativity/Innovation

Case
- Wheel Chair – B2B NPD

Session 16

Topics
- Success factors for NPD
- Across industries

Reading
- Ernst, H. 'Success factors of NPD: a review of empirical literature.' International Journal of Management Reviews

Video
- DNA of World's Innovative companies

Session 17

Topics
- New service development – Perspectives

Video
- Understand service pricing

Case
- E Bay-New technology service development

Session 18

Topics
- Best Practices-Product Development Management Association
- Learning from new product failures

Reading
- Hlavacek. J, Maxwell, C and Williams, J. *'Learn from New Product Failures,'* Industrial Research Institute
- Barczak, G. and Griffin. A. *'Perspective: Trends and Drivers of success in NPD Practices'*: Results of 2003 PDMA Best Practices Study. Journal of product Innovation Management.

Videos
- Use Failures to grow your business
- Product development Best practices

Session 19 Topics − Public issues − Environmental needs − Morality aspect − Personal ethics Videos − The Ethics of development − Michael Porter − Innovation and Competitiveness Case − Arvind Eye Clinic-Service Industry
Session 20 Topic − B2B Innovation − NPD Framework for evaluating in B2B − B2B selling process and NPD Inputs Reading − Griffin, Abbie. "Product development cycle time for business-to-business products." *Industrial Marketing Management* 31.4 (2002): 291–304. Case − Dow Corning's Xiameter Brand: Product commoditisation and Business model innovation-B2B

Afterword

Factors that may facilitate re-entry

There could be several factors such as organisational, familial, governmental and personal – that may enable women to rejoin the workforce.

Organisational enabling factors include flexible working arrangements for women – both in terms of office timings as well as giving them the option of working from home. While this number is increasing, significant adoption of flexi working arrangement is yet to be witnessed in the Indian scenario.

Advice to management would be that organisations can also set up role models or mentors to encourage mid-career women to talk about their issues. These mentors could be women who have travelled these paths successfully and therefore are able to connect with others. It is important for companies to recognise that the career journey of women would be different from those of men, as they are playing multiple roles in their lives. They should factor this in, while charting out careers for women employees.

The second aspect of familial factors is arguably the most relevant one in the Indian context. The joint family system can provide the women with the much-needed support for child care. This also ensures that women are able to fulfil their home responsibilities through the support available there. Spouses can play an important role in the lives of women who want to rejoin the workforce. However more research is required in this area.

The third aspect of governmental intervention can go a long way in ensuring that women do not give up working completely. Long maternity breaks, running public child / elderly day care systems and allowing location flexibility for spouses to be together are some of the initiatives that the Governments can do towards this.

The last factor namely the 'personal factor' is probably the most important one. This addresses the woman's personality and her attitude – that serve as self-motivator in her wanting to come back to work. Despite organisational, familial and government intervention if the woman does not have a resolve to get back, then it is of no use. The term 'aspirational deficit' is used to describe the lack of ambition amongst qualified women especially in the face of balancing challenges in work and family responsibilities. Reading self-help books, attending seminars or workshops on this subject and interacting with counsellors increase the women's awareness on this subject. With appropriate follow up, they can gain confidence and take initiatives to resume their careers. Given the unique contribution that women can make in an organisational set-up, it is critical that the entire economic system works towards empowering her around mid life. Only this will ensure that the countries' economy marches forward with the adequate utilisation of the huge resource pool available i.e women.

References

- Aisenbrey, S., Evertsson, M., & Grunow, D. (2009). Is there a career penalty for mothers' time out? A comparison of Germany, Sweden and the United States. *Social Forces, 88*(2), 573–605.
- Altman, Y., Simpson, R., Baruch, Y. & Burke, R. (2005). Refraining the 'glass ceiling' debate, in Burke, R. (Ed.) Supporting Women's Career Advancement
- Brady, D. (2004, November 8). Hopping on board the daddy track. Business Week, 3907, 100.
- Brown, A., Bimrose, J., Barnes, S. A., & Hughes, D. (2012). The role of career adaptabilities for mid-career changers. *Journal of Vocational Behavior, 80*(3), 754–761.
- Burke, R., & Vinnicombe, S. (2005) Advancing Women's careers. *Career development International, 10*, 165–167
- Cabrera, E. F. (2007). Opting out and opting in: understanding the complexities of women's career transitions. *Career Development International, 12*(3), 218–237.
- Corporate Executive Board (CEB). 2014. Four imperatives to increase representation of women in leadership positions (Arlington, VA).
- Eby, L. T., Butts, M., & Lockwood, A. (2003). Predictors of success in the era of the boundaryless career. *Journal of Organisational Behavior, 24*(6), 689–708.
- Grady, G., & McCarthy, A. M. (2008). Work-life integration: Experiences of mid-career professional working mothers. *Journal of Managerial Psychology, 23*(5), 599–622.

- Hofmeister, H., Blossfeld, H. P., & Mills, M. (2006). Globalization, uncertainty, and women's mid-career life courses, a theoretical framework. *Globalization, uncertainty and women's careers: An international comparison*, 3–31.
- Lalande, V. M., Crozier, S. D., & Davey, H. (2000). Women's Career Development and Relationships: A Qualitative Inquiry. *Canadian Journal of Counselling, 34*(3), 193–203.
- Lämsä, A. M., & Hiillos, M. (2008). Career counselling for women managers at mid-career: Developing an autobiographical approach. *Gender in Management: An International Journal, 23*(6), 395–408.
- Loscocco, K., & Smith-Hunter, A., (2004) "Women home-based business owners: insights from comparative analyses", *Women in Management Review, 19 (3),*164–173,
- Mainiero, L. A., & Sullivan, S. E. (2005). Kaleidoscope careers: An alternative explanation for the "opt-out" revolution. *Academy of Management Executive, 19*, 106–122
- Panda, A., & Gupta, R.(2007). Call for developing indigenous organization theories in India: setting agenda for future *International Journal of Indian Culture and Business Management, 1 (1–2),* 205-243
- Pompper, D. (2011). Fifty years later: Mid-career women of color against the glass ceiling in communications organizations. *Journal of Organizational Change Management, 24*(4), 464–486.
- Rajesh, S., Founder-President, A. C. C., Gruhaa, U., & Neelangarai, C. (2013). Second career of women professionals in India: A corporate perspective. *Asian Journal Of Management Research, 4*(1), 21.
- Rhodes, S. R., & Doering, M. (1983). An integrated model of career change. *Academy of Management Review, 8*(4), 631–639.
- Sullivan, S. E., & Baruch, Y. (2009). Advances in career theory and research: A critical review and agenda for future exploration. *Journal of management, 35*(6), 1542–1571.
- Sullivan, S. E., & Mainiero, L. (2008). Using the kaleidoscope career model to understand the changing patterns of women's careers: Designing HRD programs that attract and retain women. *Advances in Developing Human Resources, 10*(1), 32–49.
- White, B. (1995). The career development of successful women. *Women in Management Review, 10*(3), 4–15.
- Yang, J. L. (2005). Goodbye to all that. Fortune, 152, 169–171.

Webliography

- http://www.apprise.ox.ac.uk/academic_career_paths/
- https://www.insidehighered.com/advice/on_the_fence/essay_on_the_flaws_of_becoming_a_visiting_professor
- http://www.sciencemag.org/careers/features/2006/02/faculty-positions-tale-two-systems-tenure-v-adjunct
- https://www.nro.nl/wp-content/uploads/2014/09/Artikel-Leraar-leerlingrelaties-%E2%80%93-Helma-Koomen-ea.pdf
- http://economictimes.indiatimes.com/news/company/corporate-trends
- https://www.economist.com/blogs/democracyinamerica/2015/01/women-and-work
- http://www.forbesindia.com/blog/business-strategy/why-indian-women-leave-the-workforce/
- http://www.businesstoday.in/magazine/cover-story/business-management-teachers-in-indian-industry/story/17923.html
- https://hbr.org/2015/05/getting-more-women-into-senior-management
- http://indiatoday.intoday.in/education/story/boost-gender-diversity/1/883242.html
- https://hbr.org/2014/08/why-women-dont-apply-for-jobs-unless-theyre-100-qualified
- http://www.catalyst.org/knowledge/women-labour-force-india
- https://www.glamour.com/story/women-barriers-ceo
- https://www.wsj.com/articles/sheryl-sandberg-when-women-get-stuck-corporate-america-gets-stuck-1443600325

- https://www.youtube.com/watch?v=AlaZqdEiCbE
- https://www.youtube.com/watch?v=F9b0fi7p3Ts
- https://www.theatlantic.com/magazine/archive/2016/04/quit-your-job/471501/
- https://www.theatlantic.com/business/archive/2016/12/opting-out/500018/

www.ingramcontent.com/pod-product-compliance
Lightning Source LLC
Chambersburg PA
CBHW020910180526
45163CB00007B/2701